"*From Pandemic to Renewal* is a timely and powerful book. Writing beautifully, persuasively, and vulnerably as he shares his own life experience, Chris Rice invites us into disciplines that help us learn to see and thus know the world in which we live. Only such seeing shaped by a lively spiritual and moral imagination can renew us, the church, and our world."

Emmanuel Katongole, priest, professor, and pilgrim

"'For the first time in the eight decades since World War II, the entire world has been affected by the same devastating crisis at the same time.' These words written by Chris Rice highlight the unique moment we have journeyed through. But this moment—in a culture that quickly and mindlessly moves on—requires sustained reflection on the ways the global pandemic has shaped and continues to shape our lives. With clarity of vision and actionable practices, Chris powerfully explores the ways we are globally connected as well as the opportunities for renewal that are before us. This is a book we all need, every single one of us."

Rich Villodas, lead pastor of New Life Fellowship and author of *The Deeply Formed Life*

"This is a book of honest, truth-seeking stories and practices emerging from and leading to a life of spiritual alertness. In a time when many of us are going numb, with consequences that can only be fatal on a massive scale, Chris Rice is throwing us a lifeline. Read this book slowly, in the company of others, to explore how the personal, relational, political, and structural dimensions of essential change connect for each one of us."

Ellen F. Davis, Amos Ragan Kearns Distinguished Professor of Bible and Practical Theology at Duke Divinity School

"In this time of heightened turbulence, we sense that the world has irrevocably changed. And perhaps we have changed too: we feel unsettled and uneasy. In *From Pandemic to Renewal*, Chris Rice charts a course to embrace the disruption. We can't evade or outrun the pain, but in making the choice to move closer to it, we may paradoxically find the key to rebuilding what's broken, navigating disagreements without demonization, and addressing our world's biggest challenges with love. Chris believes there's never been a better time to make meaningful progress and seek the healing and by the time you've finished this book, y

Peter Greer, president and CEO of HOPE Inter
Mission Drift

"Chris Rice provides a way forward for those desiring to be a witness for Christ. He provides the mindset for those desiring to make their faith practical to the world around them. Do not read this alone; invite others to take the journey with you."

Alvin Sanders, president and CEO of World Impact and author of *Uncommon Church*

"Chris Rice offers deep wisdom drawn as a widely read, engaged minister of reconciliation with broad regional, national, and global experience to help leaders and readers move *From Pandemic to Renewal*. Rather than another recitation of statistics and struggles, this book illustrates how the global Covid-19 pandemic exposed existing fractures and accelerated fast-moving changes. While many have been lost in lament, Rice seeks to help us remember that Christians do not grieve as those who have no hope. His vulnerability invites readers to enter his story with our stories, and his vision inspires us to lean in faith toward where God is leading. The practices Rice proposes can help us to overcome the pressures of the pandemic, find rest in the risen Christ, and find the strength to serve well."

David Emmanuel Goatley, president of Fuller Seminary and professor of theology and ministry

"In the midst of crisis, the church finds an opportunity. My friend Chris Rice has written a text that shines the moral lens of our Christian faith on the complex social reality we find ourselves in as a church. Chris offers a compelling and hopeful vision of how spiritual practices can provide the power and opportunity for Christian witness. Chris offers the possibility of hope even in these challenging times."

Soong-Chan Rah, Robert Munger Professor of Evangelism at Fuller Theological Seminary and author of *Prophetic Lament*

Chris Rice

From Pandemic to Renewal

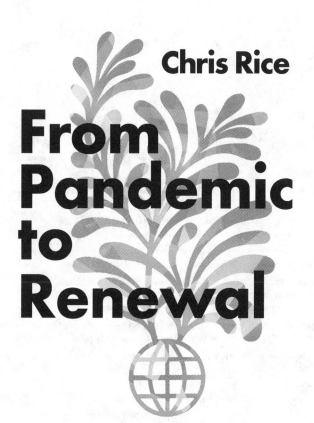

Practices for a World Shaken by Crisis

An imprint of InterVarsity Press
Downers Grove, Illinois

InterVarsity Press
P.O. Box 1400 | Downers Grove, IL 60515-1426
ivpress.com | email@ivpress.com

InterVarsity Press® is the publishing division of InterVarsity Christian Fellowship/USA®. For more information,
visit intervarsity.org.

Scripture quotations, unless otherwise noted, are from The Holy Bible, English Standard Version,
copyright © 2001 by Crossway Bibles, a division of Good News Publishers. Used by permission.
All rights reserved.

While any stories in this book are true, some names and identifying information may have been changed
to protect the privacy of individuals.

The epigraph in chapter one is from the poem "Primary Wonder" by Denise Levertov, from *Sands of the Well*,
copyright ©1994, 1995, 1996 by Denise Levertov. Reprinted by permission of New Directions Publishing Corp.

The publisher cannot verify the accuracy or functionality of website URLs used in this book beyond the date
of publication.

Cover design: David Fassett
Cover images: © CSA Images / Getty Images 131584305 and 131667735
Interior design: Daniel van Loon

ISBN 978-1-5140-0552-1 (print) | ISBN 978-1-5140-0553-8 (digital)

Printed in the United States of America ∞

Library of Congress Cataloging-in-Publication Data
Names: Rice, Chris, 1960- author.
Title: From pandemic to renewal : practices for a world shaken by crisis /
  Chris Rice.
Description: Downers Grove, IL : IVP Books, [2023] | Includes
  bibliographical references.
Identifiers: LCCN 2022052770 (print) | LCCN 2022052771 (ebook) | ISBN
  9781514005521 (print) | ISBN 9781514005538 (digital)
Subjects: LCSH: COVID-19 (Disease)–Religious aspects–Christianity. |
  COVID-19 Pandemic, 2020–Political aspects–United States. |
  Suffering–Biblical teaching.
Classification: LCC BT162.C68 R53 2023 (print) | LCC BT162.C68 (ebook) |
  DDC 261.8/321962414–dc23/eng/20230124
LC record available at https://lccn.loc.gov/2022052770
LC ebook record available at https://lccn.loc.gov/2022052771

30 29 28 27 26 25 24 23 | 12 11 10 9 8 7 6 5 4 3 2 1

To Donna,

in gratitude for adventures and

renewals beyond all we imagined

Contents

Renewing a Shaken World

Before and after. It makes for the best of stories. A crisis, followed by a journey into the unknown of who we will become.

The death of a loved one who changed your life. A sudden cancer diagnosis. Losing a job. A divorce. A bitter fight with a friend or family member. After each crisis, the future hangs in limbo, awaiting an answer from us.

In *The Lion King*, before young Simba's father, Mufasa, is killed, and after, when Simba wanders in search of his identity. In *Breaking Bad*, Walter White before his lung cancer crisis and after, the milquetoast chemistry teacher turning into a meth dealer. In *Star Wars*, before Luke Skywalker hears from Darth Vader, "I am your father," and after.

I remember the dreamy days at US airports before 2001. You could park your car at the curb, stroll inside to the arrival gate, and greet someone with a hug and flowers as they stepped off the plane. Get to the airport just an hour ahead of departure, grab lunch and a coffee, and banter with friendly strangers before your flight.

All that changed after the September 11, 2001, attacks on the United States. The term *9/11* entered the national vocabulary. Endless security lines became the new norm. US wars in Afghanistan and Iraq, the rise of al-Qaeda, civil war in Syria, and with these wars, a global migration crisis of tens of millions of people. The 2001 attacks permanently changed the world and our everyday lives. They mark a before-and-after moment in history we call "post-9/11."

In late 2019 another crisis marked life as before and after.

In the fall of that year, my wife, Donna, and I moved to New York City. To our surprise, we quickly fell in love with the city and its hustle and bustle. Crowded streets. Broadway shows. Central Park. Restaurants with food from everywhere in the world. For me, work with an international faith-based agency engaging the United Nations, with a splendid view from my office to the iconic UN building across the street. For Donna, a nursing job in Manhattan. For both of us, a new church in Queens, with members from over seventy countries.

Then, in December, came word from Wuhan, China, of a strange virus. I remember listening to a US health expert on the radio. "The virus won't come here," he said confidently. "The US has the best disease-prevention system in the world."

But by April, eight hundred people were dying every day in New York City from Covid-19. Our new city suddenly became the epicenter of the largest US health crisis in a century, and Queens, where we live, became the epicenter of the epicenter. As the United Nations shut down, I watched battles unfold between the United States and China that prevented a unified global response to the pandemic. In calls with colleagues across the world, I was alarmed to hear that none of the fifty countries where we serve was untouched by the virus.

For Donna, she was suddenly living the fear and unknown of a frontline health care worker, taking empty subways into eerily quiet streets, their silence broken only by ambulances and sirens. In the wealthiest country in the world, in its biggest and one of its wealthiest cities, she was serving Covid-19 patients, transforming trash bags into personal protective equipment. She held cellphones to the ears of dying patients to hear last words from loved ones. She loaded the dead into body bags and moved them into a makeshift morgue as she prayed for their souls. As she left work, she heard the grateful applause of New Yorkers from their apartment windows, thanking her and other frontline workers. Returning home every night, she feared she had caught the deadly virus.

OUR NEW ERA

For me and Donna, for you, for every person on this planet, we each have our own story and experience of the pandemic and the crises that came with it. This time has tested and tried us all. In our nations, communities, schools, families, and places of worship, the pandemic exposed what had been hidden, and accelerated shifts that had already begun. But I think especially of those who read this book in grief, having lost loved ones to Covid-19.

The pandemic permanently changed the world and our everyday lives, and will change the course of history. Indeed, we are living in a new pandemic era. Its effects will linger for decades, and the shocks and changes have opened a new time in our world. There was life before the pandemic, and life after, which becomes a new normal and is never quite the same. And now we face a time of decision about what kind of people we will choose to become.

This book is about seeing deeply into the challenges of our new era, and about that time of decision facing each of us.

Many other books give detailed information about the science and spread of Covid-19, the debate about its origins, the stories of devastation and loss that people experienced, the battles about countermeasures and lockdowns, and the search for a vaccine. But this book is about a far bigger picture. I use a moral lens and the lens of Scripture and Christian faith to take a deep look into how our lives and country and world are changing in this new era. This book is about seeing the new challenges that face us and the new opportunities we have for fresh growth and renewal. Most of all, I hope reading this book will foster renewal in your own life.

The pandemic and what it exposed is the crisis of a century. But this book is about how this new time is also the opportunity of a century. In order to seize the opportunity, we have to see the time clearly.

THE PANDEMIC X-RAY

In this book, we will engage this new time and opportunity through three critical themes of great relevance for our lives.

The first critical theme is what the pandemic x-ray exposed. Through a burst of radiation, an x-ray creates pictures of the inside of the body. The images show parts of the body in shades of black and white—bones, tissues, lungs, organs. An x-ray can spot not only broken bones but also pneumonia, breast cancer, tumors, and infections. An x-ray exposes what has been hidden, what we did not know and did not see about ourselves. It reveals what is healthy and what is not.

More than a crisis, the pandemic worked like an x-ray to expose the good, the bad, and the ugly in our lives, and in America, the church, and the world. Following is a brief glimpse of some of the x-ray results that present great new challenges to our lives, communities, and churches.

Anxiety and stress. Before the pandemic x-ray, we knew that parenting, marriage, and the workplace are not a walk in the park, and that young people face a far more challenging world than their parents did. Then came month after month of Covid-19 lockdowns, isolation, household bubbles, stress, and trauma. Gallup's 2022 *Global Emotions Report* said that in 2021 "negative emotions—the aggregate of the stress, sadness, anger, worry and physical pain that people feel every day"—reached a new record in the history of their tracking.[1] And in fall 2020 the American Psychological Association warned that "we are facing a national mental health crisis that could yield serious health and social consequences for years to come."[2]

Politics. Before the pandemic x-ray, politics in America were divided. But the 2020 year of pandemic and election crisis revealed an even more dangerous partisan cancer ripping the country apart—and churches too.

Digital media. Before the x-ray, life was becoming more and more digital, improving many aspects of life. *Zoom*, a verb before Covid, became a capitalized noun, and many of us are becoming connected virtually to people in ways we never imagined before. Yet the pandemic also exposed sinister forces in a new age in which the algorithms of global tech giants like Facebook, Twitter, and Google often rule how we see the world.

Class and race. Before the x-ray, many disputed the facts of social disparity. Yet the pandemic saw food banks overwhelmed as the Dow Jones Industrial Average hit an all-time high. We witnessed the disproportionate Covid-19 deaths of black, Latino, and Native Americans. A growing chasm was exposed between two worlds of work—white-collar workers safely teleworking from home as delivery workers dropped dinner at their doorstep. Prepandemic, I never heard Asian Americans talk about carefully planning travel routes, buying mace for self-protection, or being afraid to walk down a street. Because of an alarming rise in anti-Asian violence, that changed.

Pandemics are a new reality. Before the x-ray, most of us didn't even know what a pandemic was. But whether we live in Kansas City, Caracas, Kigali, or Kyoto, all of us now share a new global experience and language of closed borders, lockdowns, face masks, social distancing, testing, and vaccines. We all recognize the iconic spiky blob of the deadly coronavirus, and we know the fears and anger and prejudices a crisis like this reveals in our hearts and minds. We have all experienced the human toll, the disruption of "normal," and an unknown future. Not only have we faced the monster, but we have learned that new and devastating diseases are emerging in people every year, any one of which has the potential to spread globally.[3] And along with this potential, further tests of our character, communities, and churches continue in this new time.

Once these x-ray results are in, we process it and decide our course of action. In this book, we will explore positive pathways for navigating these new realities and challenges.

OUR FUTURE IS JOINED TO OTHERS'

The second critical theme this book will engage is how we are facing the global crisis of a century. This is of great relevance for our lives.

There have been many crises in our world in recent years. A massive earthquake in Haiti. The migration of millions of refugees from Syria. A tsunami and nuclear disaster in Fukushima, Japan. Racial reckoning in the United States following the murder of George Floyd. The Russian military invasion of

Ukraine. All are devastating before-and-after moments in those countries.

But unlike other crises, the pandemic has touched every person on this planet. *For the first time in the eight decades since World War II, the entire world has been affected by the same devastating crisis at the same time.* As Covid-19 spread rapidly across the world in 2020 and beyond, and as so many have died, along with this has come economic loss, fear, polarization, death, and grief. From indigenous people in the remote village of Mangual in the Peruvian Amazon jungle to executives on Wall Street in New York, no life has gone untouched and unchanged.

Yet this crisis of a century shared by every person on our planet has also revealed a truth that can change our lives. It shows that we are joined to other human beings in this world in ways we have largely overlooked. Speaking to a Christian audience, theologian Stanley Hauerwas put it this way:

> The pandemic revealed that we are bound to one another around the world in a way that how Christians fare in China makes a good deal of difference for how we fare in North Carolina. And that we are joined in a common life that gives us a sense of obligation to one another. That doesn't mean that we are not also bound to those who do not claim to be Christian. We are all creatures of a good God.[4]

In this new time in our world, our future depends on becoming more joined to others, across divides, in spite of challenges that create borders between people and block better solutions—from red-blue political divides, to racial and economic problems, to our own divided selves, and to the reality that, in these days, many find it harder to talk about difficult issues with their own family or church members than anyone else. We face many global challenges today, such as pandemics, changes in climate, and conflicts that cross borders. These border-crossing problems are shared by all human beings and cannot be solved locally or nationally. To faithfully engage border-creating and border-crossing problems requires border-crossing people. Becoming such people is a special identity and task given by our Lord for such a time as this, and a major theme we will explore.

AN OPPORTUNITY FOR RENEWAL

A third critical theme engaged in this book is how this new time is the opportunity of a century. We prefer not to face shocks and crises. Yet they can create an unprecedented opportunity for clarity and renewal in our lives.

In the winter of 2013, my work at Duke Divinity School in North Carolina was hit by an organizational crisis. I worked tirelessly to solve the problems but could find no answers. Full of anxiety, many nights I couldn't sleep.

To get some perspective, I decided to go to a retreat center called St. Francis Springs. The entire drive I wrestled with the crisis. When I arrived, I met other retreatants who came to pray. But I went out into the woods, desperate to find cellphone reception. There I was, next to the prayer labyrinth, texting and calling as if I was on the floor of the New York Stock Exchange. I was there to *fix*.

The next day I decided to talk to the retreat center's founder, Father Louie, a Franciscan priest. "Maybe he can give me some insight," I thought. That night, at the end of another day trying to solve the crisis, I met with Father Louie.

For thirty minutes, I poured out my heart and soul to him—the criticisms, the turmoil, the problems insoluble, the pain, the complexity. I finished and turned to Father Louie for advice.

And these were his first words: "Chris, what an opportunity!"

What an opportunity. Are you kidding me? That sounded like a salesman, not a spiritual sage.

"Chris," he said, "Why are you here? Are you here to fix your problems at Duke? Are you here to make calls and send emails? This crisis is a gift. God is revealing many things about you and your institution and your life you would not otherwise see. But you need to slow down to see them."

The next morning, I woke up and, with fear and trembling, put away my computer and cellphone. I went out into the surrounding land and forest and began walking. It was winter. The sky was gray. The ground was cold. All was brown and barren. There were no leaves on the trees. My heart, too, was cold. And I kept walking. Listening. Watching.

As I walked, as I slowed down, I began to notice something I hadn't seen before. I was surrounded by life. Yes, it was winter, but in that barren landscape, I realized that spring was underground, making its way upward and outward. Instead of only death, I began to see life.

Over the next several days, no circumstance changed. But I saw my life situation with different eyes.

When I returned to our home in Durham, Donna and I began a conversation that opened an unexpected new highway in our life. I came to believe that solving the crisis at Duke did not have my name on it. Donna came to believe that she was open to a whole new chapter. Both of us were restless, ready for a new adventure. Next came a series of steps we could not have planned. A year later, we were living in South Korea, serving as codirectors of a Christian agency's work in Northeast Asia, including guiding humanitarian work in North Korea. Growing up as a missionary kid in South Korea, I had never thought it would be possible to fulfill a life-long dream: to cross into North Korea and, in the name of Christ, pursue peace on both sides of the divided peninsula. There was madness to the move, and many challenges came with it, from financial to family. But great growth came as well.

"What an opportunity!" Father Louie had said. Looking back now, what an opportunity indeed. Those days of interruption, silence, and reflection became a decisive before-and-after moment in my life. They brought clarity about what I was and was not called to do, led me and Donna to reevaluate our careers, and opened up a new adventure of growth and service for us.

Even in the barren times of winter in our lives, growth is at work, is present, in hidden ways. The pandemic and the challenges it has revealed is not only the crisis of a century. It is also the opportunity of a century—an opportunity to clarify our priorities and to seek renewal in our lives and world. Renewal doesn't require moving to another place, changing careers, or dropping out of school. But seizing the opportunity does require some slowing down.

It is often said that we learn from experience. But in today's fast world of constant communication and information, we are overloaded with experiences. No, we don't learn from experience. We learn from reflection on experience. A crisis can lead to decline in our lives, but if we are willing to put aside our distracted busyness and listen to it, a crisis can become an opportunity to release fresh vision, energy, and renewal.

THE PATHWAY OF THIS BOOK

I want to slow down to reflect together, to look deeply into and learn from this new and unprecedented time that will permanently change our lives and communities. We will explore eight great challenges posed by our new world. With each challenge I offer a transformative practice. Whether one is making pottery, playing a video game, or learning contemplative prayer, becoming excellent in our pursuits requires forming new habits and disciplines, repeated over and over. Gradually those fresh patterns form us into different people. That is what I mean by a practice. We will explore how these practices are a source of renewal, a means of grace, a pathway to becoming more like Christ—and, along the way, I hope to expand our understanding of what renewal is and how it happens.

Each chapter explores one challenge that has emerged in this new time, as well as one practice for responding to that challenge, providing a pathway of hope and transformation:

- Bearing joy for a world of frantic anxiety
- Centering the vulnerable for a world of rising disparity
- Being peacemakers for a world of surging polarization
- Redeeming power for a world of political mediocrity
- Making transnational disciples for a world of American blinders
- Pursuing private integrity for a world of public validation
- Cultivating moral imagination for a world of unprecedented dangers
- Renewing the church for a world longing for hope

With each challenge and practice, we will not take a long swim, but a deep dive. We will explore how these eight practices enliven our witness as we apply them in our lives, churches, and communities, and how they collectively offer a pathway to personal and social renewal in this new era. While we are in uncharted territory now, at the same time, many of these challenges are not new. But they have accelerated and become more serious, and have exposed idols the church is tolerating that have greatly weakened Christian life. Drawing on wisdom from the past is even more urgent now.

MY MINISTRY CONTEXT

As I share with you, I will draw on a lifetime of experiences that speak into the present time of opportunity.

My perspective and stories come from journeys across many cultures, contexts, and churches: I was born in the United States but grew up in South Korea at a time of military dictatorship, economic turbulence, and church growth. I lived for seventeen years in inner city Jackson, Mississippi, serving in a multiracial church and community development organization. For ten years, I served as cofounding director of the Duke Divinity School Center for Reconciliation, working to nourish students and Christian leaders to heal divides in the United States and East Africa. For five years, Donna and I were based in South Korea, serving together as corepresentatives for Northeast Asia with the Mennonite Central Committee (MCC)—a one-hundred-year-old, international, faith-based agency working in more than fifty countries, pursuing "relief, development, and peace, in the name of Christ." During those years, I led many MCC teams into North Korea. Finally, I bring the perspective of my recent years of advocacy and diplomacy work in New York City, serving as director of MCC's UN office. From neighborhood work across racial and economic divides in Mississippi, to a front-row seat at the United Nations, to the divides I've experienced in my own heart and relationships, I hope that my story will connect with and speak to yours as we seek God's pathways of renewal toward the future.

At the same time, I recognize my social location as a white American male with a doctoral degree. For those who carry massive debt, who are unemployed, who struggle with health issues, who face America from the margins, renewal may sound like a privileged posture to take. What I hope to show in this book is that the heart of renewal includes a reversal of what is often seen as the "center," and that visions of change that do not include all people—especially the most vulnerable—are not the renewal that God seeks. The Bible is a story of God's renewal coming to and originating from the most unlikely places.

THE TIME THAT IS GIVEN TO US

One of my favorite before-and-after stories is *The Lord of the Rings* by J. R. R. Tolkien. The gentle hobbit named Frodo leads a quiet life as one of the "little people" of the earth. After he is given the Ring of Power, he journeys with friends into a land of darkness, and the Ring's grip of control slowly overtakes him.

During a time of crisis, Frodo turns to his mentor, Gandalf. "I wish it need not have happened in my time," he says. "So do I," said Gandalf, "and so do all who live to see such times. But that is not for them to decide. All we have to decide is what to do with the time that is given us."[5]

I imagine that you, like me, have wished many times that such a time of crisis had never happened in our time. Yet in this new era, we must decide what we will do with the time we have been given.

A before-and-after crisis makes for the best of stories because it reveals who we truly are, introduces a time of decision that will determine who we will become, and offers an opportunity to grow in ways we cannot imagine.

This before-and-after moment has changed the world and will reshape our lives for decades to come. But will it be for better or worse? Lying ahead is the unknown story of who each of us will become in this new world. And for followers of Christ, choices lie ahead as we face what our personal faith and public witness will become.

In this new era, as we face challenges as near as our own families and as global as the ripple effects of the superpower clash between the United States and China, the call to become new people is about God's choosing. It is not always easy or comfortable. But it ultimately brings great growth and joy. Renewal is where strange and difficult ground becomes holy ground. Let's begin the journey.

CHAPTER ONE

Bearing Joy for a World of Frantic Anxiety

And then
once more the quiet mystery
is present to me, the throng's clamor
recedes: the mystery
that there is anything, anything at all,
let alone cosmos, joy, memory, everything,
rather than void: and that, O Lord,
Creator, Hallowed one, You still,
hour by hour sustain it.

DENISE LEVERTOV, "PRIMARY WONDER"

Airplanes are a barometer of the national mood. My daughter is a flight attendant, and over the course of 2020, as Covid-19 battles, racial tensions, and election division intensified in the United States, so did her "you won't believe what happened on the plane today" texts and stories about abusive language, fights, and incidents of rudeness and defiance. As Americans took rising anger and anxiety from living rooms to airplane aisles, the term *air rage* hit the headlines as a growing threat to air travel.

Anxiety was already increasing before this time of crisis. In a 2020 book *Can't Even: How Millennials Became the Burnout*

Generation, Anne Helen Petersen writes, "Increasingly—and increasingly among millennials—burnout isn't just a temporary affliction. It's our contemporary condition."[1] Petersen speaks of US millennials mired in endless to-do lists and debt, and of digital work becoming 24/7 work and social media becoming all-consuming.

This accelerating condition of burnout and anxiety extends beyond the United States. In 2020, a video went viral in China of a student from an elite university riding his bike at night while working on a laptop perched on the handlebars. An onslaught of online photos of similarly overwhelmed and overworked students followed. Workers at large Chinese tech firms, who once referred to their long work hours as "996" (nine in the morning to nine at night, six days a week), now speak of "007" (working online twenty-four hours a day, seven days a week).

"Every age has its signature afflictions," writes Byung-Chul Han, the Korean-born, Germany-based philosopher, in *The Burnout Society*. Burnout, for Han, is depression and exhaustion. Whatever our location or walk of life, the pandemic intensified this signature affliction of our age by reducing our chance for social encounter, confining many of us to our phones, and giving us many alarming things to be anxious about.[2]

CAPTIVITY TO ACTIVITY

Han writes that our age has become captive to the illusion that "the more active one becomes, the freer one is." One wonders: If not by action, then how will we address the challenges of this pandemic era? But seeing more activism as more freedom is a captivity that I have struggled with over many years.

Earlier in my life I lived in Jackson, Mississippi, as part of a multiracial church and community development organization called Voice of Calvary. I became close with a black Mississippian named Spencer Perkins (his father, civil rights activist Rev. John Perkins, founded the organization). Spencer and I wrote a book called *More Than Equals* and created a national platform to promote racial justice and reconciliation. We lived in an under-resourced neighborhood at the margins, worshiped across racial and economic lines, and worked for change at the grassroots. With others, our families shared daily life in an intentional Christian community called Antioch. Our homes and lives were open to hospitality—from welcoming neighborhood teenagers to single mothers to men just out of prison. At Antioch we had a saying, "there's always room for one more at the dinner table."

At the heart of our life and vision, and of Spencer's and my teaching, was Jesus' story of the Good Samaritan who crosses social divides to "prove neighbor" to the stranger at the side of the road who has been unjustly treated (Luke 10:25-37). Activists at heart, we got a lot right. Our motto, you might say, was "yes, we can."

But after twelve years together, we were in crisis. Our Antioch community had shriveled up inside, riddled by unresolved relational difficulties, financial stress, and overwork. Even more, Spencer's and my relationship had eroded. While he and I were traveling the nation preaching about justice and reconciliation, we could hardly sit at the same dinner table at our Antioch community. Our lists of each other's sins began to grow: "You did this to me." "Well that's because you did that to me." "Well you did that to me . . ."

The deep friendship and partnership Spencer and I had forged was on the verge of breaking up. Facing the intensity of our 24/7 common life and work, many of us had run out of vision, energy, and spiritual resources to go on. In my view, "yes, we can" had become a gospel of trying harder and doing more. And that did not feel like good news. We were exhausted. The joy was gone. We were in crisis. But we had no idea how to be liberated from our captivity to activity.

John Calvin once wrote, "For what is idolatry if not this: to worship the gifts in place of the Giver himself?" Activism is a gift. But extreme activism as an end in itself can make an idol of our indispensability, replacing the Only Indispensable One—the Giver.[3]

THE CHALLENGE OF TRAUMA

The story of our Mississippi crisis is a lens that helps us see three challenges facing our anxious and exhausted era, our burnout society.

The first is the challenge of trauma. Because of our Mississippi community's location at America's margins, our work of hospitality and justice, and our multiracial life, we lived in proximity to pain and brokenness, both external and internal. In a similar way to our Mississippi experience, the pandemic put all of us in close contact with trauma and conflict.

For some, that trauma has been physical, visceral, and even violent. More Americans have died of Covid-19 than from World War II and the Civil War—*combined*. While the suffering was hidden for many, not so for family and loved ones of those who died. The police murder of George Floyd in Minneapolis exposed patterns of violence against African Americans. As talk of a "Wuhan virus" increased, so did violent attacks against Asian Americans. All of us watched as bitter divisions over the pandemic, the 2020 election, and race tore communities and churches apart. No matter our politics, all it took was seeing headlines or opening social media to provoke further tension and anger. All these were distressing and disturbing experiences, all various forms of trauma unleashing further anxiety.

Facing trauma, the temptation is to flee or to fight by becoming more and more active. But, as with our Mississippi community, we will eventually reach a breaking point of exhaustion and mental breakdown. Healing the trauma and conflict in and around us is a marathon, not a sprint. A yes-we-can spirituality of trying harder and doing more cannot sustain us, cannot carry us over the long haul.

THE CHALLENGE OF EXCESS POSITIVITY

A second challenge from the Mississippi crisis was revealed in the root problem that began to erode our lives and work. Our problem was not pessimism or despair. Until the crisis, our lives were bustling with activity and positivity. Our welcoming communal dinner slogan said it well: "There's always room for one more."

The root problem of our age of burnout and frantic anxiety is not despair but a hyperactive life of "yes, we can." Wouldn't you think high-achievement, prosperous, yes-we-can people have more joy? Well, they don't. By any measure, the United States is the most wealthy, influential, and powerful country in the history of the world. And the United States also has the world's fourth-highest stress level.[4]

South Korea had well-deserved success in controlling the spread of the Covid-19 virus, and a can-do culture of collective cooperation for the common good helps drive the country's remarkable achievements. Indeed, just sixty years after being one of the poorest countries in the world after the Korean War, South Korea has the world's twelfth-largest economy, hosting global brand names from Samsung, Hyundai, and Kia to the boy band BTS. But the competitive drive for achievement has come at a high cost. Tragically, despite prosperity, in South Korea young people are known as the "seven-give-up generation," believing they will never find love, marriage, childbirth, close relationships, home ownership, personal dreams, or hope (in the five years my wife and I lived in South Korea [2014–2019], the "give-up" list grew from five to seven). They, along with American millennials and China's 996 generation, reflect young adults in the world who may be rejecting a kind of advancement they find meaningless.

This paradox of prosperity without joy reveals the power of philosopher Han's insight that burnout society in our global time is rooted not in negativity but the very opposite: an excess of *positivity*. Han writes that in this age of burnout, "The complaint of the depressive individual, 'Nothing is possible,' is only possible in a society that believes, 'Nothing is impossible.'"[5]

THE CHALLENGE OF ACTIVISM TURNING TO VIOLENCE

A third challenge revealed in the Mississippi crisis is how burnout breaks relationships. Deep practices of seeking justice and reconciliation were written into the daily fabric of our lives. Across racial lines, we lived in a community at the margins, talked honestly about race in our lives and in society, published a national magazine, and organized with others in a national association. Yet at the very same time, a culture of trying harder and doing more gradually began to weaken and damage our relationships, our hope, our joy.

The danger of hyperactivism turning into a form of violence never occurred to me until I encountered the writings of Trappist monk Thomas Merton. Merton wrote eloquently about the great social challenges of the 1960s—from the rise of nuclear weapons to racial injustice, from abortion to war. Yet Merton warned about an insidious threat—internal, not external—overlooked by many actively involved in changing the world: what he called "a pervasive form of contemporary violence to which the idealist most easily succumbs: activism and overwork." Merton continued,

> The rush and pressure of modern life are a form, perhaps the most common form, of its innate violence. To allow oneself to be carried away by a multitude of conflicting concerns, to surrender to too many demands, to commit oneself to too many projects, to want to help everyone in everything, is to succumb to violence. The frenzy of our activism neutralizes our work for peace. It destroys our own inner capacity for peace. It destroys the fruitfulness of our own work, because it kills the root of inner wisdom which makes work fruitful.[6]

When Han describes the affliction of today's burnout society, he sees what Merton saw, but on steroids—a world of overachievement and overcommunication that requires people to strive to the point of self-destruction. Writes Han, "It reflects a humanity waging war on itself."[7] This seems to describe the world as experienced by many young adults in the United States, South Korea, and China, a world they may be beginning to reject.

Merton teaches us that we must always analyze the quest for change through a spiritual lens. He saw that deep change requires being deeply rooted in our own spirits and hearts. Rooted in the shallow frenzy of idealism and hyperactivity alone, the fruit in our lives will be tasty for only a season, then will grow bitter and the tree eventually barren. The tree may seem strong to outside eyes, but it will gradually wither and then fall, often during a sudden crisis. This is how being rooted in overwork and frantic activism can become a form of violence to ourselves and to others, as began to happen in the growing bitterness and hurtful words and broken relationships in our Mississippi community.

THE ANTIDOTE FOR ANXIETY

Facing our time of crisis and burnout, I believe the most essential virtue is *joy*.

Joy? Given the pain of this time, shouldn't we begin with lament? With the cry of Jesus from the cross, "My God, my God, why have you forsaken me?" (Matthew 27:46).

Yet this same Jesus is the one who "for the joy set before him endured the cross" (Hebrews 12:2). In the Bible, joy does not dismiss suffering. The one crying out, the one we call Lord and whose way we follow, was one with joy deep in his bones.

The two bookends of the story of Jesus—birth and resurrection—are permeated with joy. The baby in Elizabeth leaps (Luke 1:41). The angel greets Mary with joy and Mary rejoices (Luke 1:47). The angel announces "great joy" to shepherds. The visiting Magi were "overjoyed."

Jesus' words are filled with joy. "These things I have spoken to you, that my joy may be in you, and that your joy may be full" (John 15:11). "You will weep and lament . . . but your sorrow will turn into joy" (John 16:20). He goes on to say, "But I will see you again, and your hearts will rejoice, and no one will take your joy from you" (John 16:22).

Jesus got joy deep into the bones of his disciples. After his ascension, it is said they "returned to Jerusalem with great joy, and were continually in the temple blessing God" (Luke 24:52-53).

Your favorite uplifting song, your team winning the playoff game, a meal at your favorite restaurant—there's a place for things that make us happy. Yet what we see in the story of Jesus is that happiness and joy are not the same. According to missiologist Evelyne Reisacher, biblical joy is "a delight in life that runs deeper than pain or pleasure. This kind of joy is not limited by or tied solely to external circumstances. It is not a fleeting emotion but a quality of life that can be experienced in the midst of a variety of emotions."

The antidote for anxiety is not activism. It is joy. What does it take to be rooted in joy, in "a delight in life that runs deeper than pain or pleasure"?

TRYING HARDER AND DOING MORE, INTERRUPTED

In the Bible, there is an intimate relationship between lament and joy. The beginning of liberation, the first move to a cure, is naming the condition we are in. Naming the trauma in and around us in this new era, the excess of yes-we-can positivity that gradually leads to despair, and the danger of hyper-activism breaking relationships—this is lament. Lament takes us to the depths of brokenness. Only there can we see our need for God in a way we have never experienced before. That is what happened in our Mississippi community.

In the depths of despair, we asked two mentors to fly in for a last-ditch attempt to save me and Spencer from a split-up. John and Judy Alexander had spent many years in Christian justice work. John had been the editor of *The Other Side*, the leading prophetic evangelical magazine at the time, alongside *Sojourners*. Now they were part of a small church in San Francisco.

But John and Judy didn't come to talk about justice. All they wanted to talk about was the need to give each other grace. And Spencer and I wanted no part of it. We both felt wronged. We both wanted to win. Grace didn't sound fair.

John and Judy talked to Spencer, to me, and to each Antioch member. A couple days later, we all gathered. When John gave his diagnosis of our problem, I was on the edge of my seat.

"Which does the Bible speak of more," he asked, "loving God or loving your neighbor?"

I thought it was a trick question. How can you separate the two? Jesus certainly didn't! (Matthew 22:36-40).

After watching us squirm, John chuckled and said, "I'm a very anal person." He said he had actually counted all the Bible verses about loving God and loving neighbor. They were numerous, the latter including many about the call to liberate the poor, which had shaped our Mississippi life and work profoundly.

But John said he had made a discovery: far more than texts about loving God or loving neighbor were stories about God's love for us. The most important truth in the world, said John, is not our trying harder to love God or others, but God's unconditional acts of love for us. He had a warning: "If you don't get God's love deep into your bones you will become very dangerous people. Especially activists like you."

John went on: "The most important person in this community is not any of you, or the people in the neighborhood. The most important person in any community is Jesus. Your life has to keep Jesus' love at the center."

Over the next couple days, John and Judy failed to get me and Spencer to forgive each other. Privately, I told John that I could see no option but to leave. John said something that pained me—that the conflict with Spencer was mostly my fault. And then John said something that made me pause. "Chris, maybe you need to stay, simply as an act of faith. And, by staying, to wait and see what God does." It wasn't what I wanted to hear. But it had the ring of gospel truth. Sometimes a breakthrough can only come when we feel we have come to end of our own power. Only when, in weakness, we surrender ourselves to a new and greater truth, a deeper power.

The next day I stood in our church choir as we sang the song "The Potter's House." The words penetrated into my hard heart: "You who are broken, stop by the Potter's house. You who need mending, stop by the Potter's house. The Potter wants to put you back together again." Tears welled up in my eyes. I began to feel a seeping into my bones, breaking through my pride, telling me I was beloved, that I could let go of trying to win, that I could surrender to a cup I wished not to drink from.

In the last meeting before John and Judy were to leave, still on the verge of splitting up, somehow the love that John had spoken of penetrated our stubborn bones.

Spencer had come to the meeting to give me grace to leave Antioch. "I want Chris and Donna to be happy," he said, "even if it means them leaving." And I had come to the meeting to somehow say we had found the grace to stay. And we gave each other the grace to make a new beginning.

A new reality overwhelmed our list of wrongs, and the interruption shook our life at Antioch to the core. Over the following weeks, a fresh joy came to our life. We began talking about what it would mean to replace the culture of demands with a culture of grace. Spencer said it was "like going back to kindergarten," learning a new language and new practices.

Joy, we learned, comes when we get God's love deep into our bones, and in being a community of people who find ways to do that for each other every day.[8]

HOLDING TWO STORIES TOGETHER

But another tragedy soon hit our Mississippi community that challenged our renewal of joy.

Two months after the breakthrough, Spencer and I led a major conference we had organized in Jackson. The last night, we stood side by side as we often did, giving the final conference message. We told the story of our breakthrough, and what it was teaching us about the larger quest for justice and reconciliation in America.

But just three days later, at age forty-four, Spencer died suddenly of a heart attack. One day life was normal, and the next, never the same. It was a devastating loss—for our church, for Antioch, and most of all for Spencer's family.

I was shaken with grief. But I tried to keep everything going at first. Yes-we-can is so deep in my bones. I believed I needed to keep the ministry Spencer and I started moving forward. But I was coming apart. I had to pull away.

I drove to a retreat center in northern Mississippi. I walked the grounds. Alone, full of grief under a dark night sky filled with stars, I poured out my heart.

It was there, in stillness and silence, that I came to an astounding and disturbing discovery. For the first time, I realized that during seventeen years of intense life and work in Mississippi, I had never once taken time to get away alone to cease work, be still, reflect, and pray. *Seventeen years.*

I was drawn to the story that Spencer and I told whenever we spoke, the Good Samaritan story in the Gospel of Luke (10:25-37). In response to the lawyer's question "Who is my neighbor?" Jesus tells about the outcast Samaritan on the road to Jericho, who sees and rescues a man who has been robbed and beaten. It is a story about going out of our way for the suffering stranger.

But as I read the story for the first time after Spencer's death, I saw that the Good Samaritan was not the end of the story.

Immediately after this, Luke reports that Jesus goes to Bethany, to the home of sisters Martha and Mary (10:38-42). There, with Martha so busy in the kitchen, so occupied, Mary sits in stillness at the feet of Jesus, listening to the Lord. When Martha protests, Jesus responds: "You are worried and upset about many things, but few things are needed—or indeed only one. Mary has chosen what is better, and it will not be taken away from her" (Luke 10:41-42 NIV).

The Good Samaritan story is about allowing our lives to be interrupted by injustice. "Go and do likewise" commands Jesus (Luke 10:37). We can't know Jesus without a spirituality of extravagant justice. Yet what immediately follows at Bethany is a story of radical devotion. Extravagant action cannot be separated from extravagant devotion.

THE GRAMMAR OF CHRISTIAN ACTION

Holding together the two stories of "go and do likewise" and "sitting at the Lord's feet" in Luke 10 speaks deeply to the captivity to activity in our anxious world, and roots us in the joy Jesus experienced.

Christian theology does not begin with a book (the Bible) but the person the book points to—*Jesus Christ*. Likewise, the grammar of Christian action in the world—the basic structure guiding our way of seeing the world—does not begin with an *imperative* command or demand of "do this, do that." It does not begin with the "Go and do likewise" of the Good Samaritan story. In fact it does not begin with words, but with *the Word*—with God becoming flesh and dwelling among us (John 1:14). It begins with the one saying these words, with the one who sends us, with his story, life, being, character, and identity. In other words, the grammar of Christian action in the world begins with an *indicative*, a statement of fact, a revelation, a surprising and joyful reality that is true outside of ourselves, long before we come on the scene as actors. It begins with who God is and with God's action—what God has been doing, is doing, will do.

Before "Go and do likewise," we see the grammar of Christian activism rooted earlier in Luke, with Jesus' announcement at the beginning of his public ministry: "The Spirit of the Lord is upon me because he has anointed me to preach good news to the poor" (Luke 4:18, 19). The Spirit is upon *Jesus* to do these things. This is who Jesus is, what Jesus is about to do in the world. We are not in the picture yet. Jesus has not even chosen his first disciples.

Yet this is still not the deepest roots of who Jesus is. We can take another step back in Luke, to this moment:

When all the people were being baptized, Jesus was baptized too. And as he was praying, heaven was opened and the Holy Spirit descended on him in bodily form like a dove. And a voice came from heaven: "You are my Son, whom I love; with you I am well pleased."

Now Jesus himself was about thirty years old when he began his ministry. (Luke 3:21-23 NIV)

Jesus is still. He is praying. He has not begun his public ministry. And this is the moment when God declares that Jesus, God's son, is beloved. Jesus is beloved *without doing anything*. Before he begins his public ministry of three years, Jesus spends *thirty* years in quiet and in hiddenness, becoming deeply rooted in being beloved. Jesus' stillness, his belovedness, precedes his action. And precedes our action.

The note "he was praying," and Jesus' subsequent movement into the silence and testing of the wilderness (Luke 4:1-13), suggests that he was immersed in the life of prayer. So the indicative (who Jesus is, rooted in being beloved, in being anointed to preach good news to the poor) is still not followed by Jesus' imperative ("Go and do likewise"), but by the *optative* (expressing a desire)—in other words, Jesus' response being rooted was prayer. We express the optative when we're on our knees, pouring out our wishes and feelings and laments and praise to God. So the grammar is "God, since you are one who loves this world, who liberates the poor, who sets the prisoner free, will you please do something? Fill us with your belovedness and form us into ones who join you in bringing good news to the poor!" Deeply rooted in the indicative and the optative, we respond to the imperative: "Go and do likewise."

When the imperative takes control of our lives—the demand, the must, the have to—that becomes captivity to activity. But when the indicative and optative take precedence, we live and act rooted in Jesus' belovedness, and in our being beloved by Jesus without doing anything. In the words of John Alexander, we move with the love of God deep in our bones. This, then, is the grammar of Christian action: before we *do* we are *sent*, before we are sent we are *still*, before we are still we are already *beloved*. Following this Christ-centered pattern, the difference

Christian action makes in the world comes from being deeply rooted in being beloved, being still, and being sent.

What does it look like to live and act rooted in that kind of joy? In Jesus' joy? In being deeply rooted in being beloved, being still, and being sent? Let's turn to that now.

PRACTICES OF BEARING JOY

Business magnate Bill Gates once said, "Just in terms of allocation of time resources, religion is not very efficient. There's a lot more I could be doing on a Sunday morning."[9] Gates was right. Mary's stillness and extravagant devotion in Luke 10 is out of place, even scandalous, in a world of frantic activity and achievement. As novelist Flannery O'Connor once wrote, "All human nature vigorously resists grace because grace changes us and the change is painful."[10] For those of us living in captivity to activity, rooting ourselves in practices of joy and belovedness doesn't come easily.

After Spencer passed away, a new chapter opened for our family; we moved from Mississippi to small-town Vermont, where my parents lived, for a time of rest. I exchanged multiracial life for the whitest state in America. Instead of Antioch's communal dinner table of twenty, it was just our family of five. Instead of important meetings to go to and crises to attend to, there was Cub Scouts and a stillness broken only by singing chickadees.

Seventeen years of intense activism didn't prepare me for this. My habits looked as if the psalmist had said "Be *busy* and know that I am God." Depression set in. It can be disturbing when the yardstick you have always used to measure your significance, even your devotion to God, is suddenly challenged.

Yet those months of dissonance in Vermont became a time of learning to be like Mary, to be still.

This new time in our country and culture is the opportunity of a century for deep renewal, and that renewal will not be rooted in efficiency but in joy. Still, if joy is the most essential virtue, it may also be the most elusive. I want to share three practices with you that have helped me bear joy.

CONTEMPLATIVE RHYTHMS

As I mentioned, the church I attend now, New Life Fellowship, is in Queens, which was the epicenter of Covid-19 in New York City and is known as the most ethnically diverse urban area in the world. One of New Life's core values is being multiracial and committed to racial justice. Yet what also drew Donna and me to this church in the rough and tumble of Queens is another value they consider equally important—what they call "being monastic." New Life pastor and author Rich Villodas says this means being rooted in contemplative rhythms. He explains that while the object of mindfulness is "often better psychological and physical health (very important things)," the object of contemplative rhythms is a person—that is, its object is communion with God. And the core of that communion "is the commitment to establish relationship with God based on friendship rather than demands."[11]

One contemplative rhythm that keeps me rooted in joy instead of demands is regular times at retreat centers and monasteries. In fact, a friend of mine, who teaches political science at Duke University, likes to joke that "Chris Rice retreats more than the French army." That is certainly a milestone I never expected to achieve. Yes, I flee! Now with delight! I flee from all the noise that poses as urgent importance and seeks to become dictator of my life. Indeed, I have learned that I must take at least two nights away, because I need the first twenty-four hours to "detox" from that noise. In stillness I come to the realization, time and time again, how my life has become a mile wide in frantic activity and an inch deep in clarity, peacefulness, and effectiveness.

In the practice of the sabbath, another contemplative rhythm, *Burnout Society* author Han describes a surprising antidote to the affliction of our age:

> The Sabbath, too—a word that originally meant *stopping*—is a day of not to . . . a day free of all *in-order-to*, of all care. It is a matter of interval. After He created it, God declared the Seventh Day holy. That is, the day of in-order-to is not sacred, but rather the day of not-to, a day on which the *use of the useless* proves possible. It is a day of tiredness . . . a time without work, a time of, and for, play . . . a time of peace. Tiredness is disarming.[12]

Wasn't Mary's sitting at the feet of Jesus a bit "useless"? Isn't this time wasted, time that could be better spent controlling and influencing people and events directly? It depends on your theory of change. "Not-to" rhythms of sabbath, silence, prayer, and stillness root us in being beloved by a person rather than achievement and demands. In the face of so much to be done, when we cease and desist to pray, worship, rest, recreate, and feast, we declare that there really is a difference between God's endless love and ours, between God's action in the world and ours. And that returns us to the joy that Thomas Merton called "the root of inner wisdom which makes work fruitful." I, for one, can testify that developing those new rhythms changed my life as much as my years in Mississippi did.

As Bill Gates observed, contemplative rhythms are not efficient. But they do slow us down to catch up with God.

SPARKING JOY

Slowing down may look like reassessing what's keeping us busy and rushed, what's filling up our lives to the exclusion of rest and enjoyment. Perhaps you've heard of Marie Kondo, the cheerful host of the TV show *Tidying Up*. Kondo is invited into homes to help Americans declutter their lives. She gently guides families to reassess all their belongings, keep only items that "spark joy," and give away the rest. Through this practice, she helps people see a deeper vision of simplicity: centering life in what relates to joy and need. Yet people in the show often have trouble letting go of the space-filling clutter they've become attached to, and face grief in letting go of that which has become dear yet somehow blocks their growth.

It is easy for our lives to become cluttered by many things that stand in the way of the things that spark true joy.

After Spencer passed away, I met with a grief counselor. At one point I told her about all that had to be done to keep alive the national organization that Spencer and I had founded—finances, staff, programs, properties. She stopped me short with a question: "Chris, what idea of the future fills your heart with joy?"

My comeback was quick. "But you don't understand. You don't know all that I am responsible for."

She said, "Yes, but those are details. God will take care of them. Keep your focus on the bigger picture."

After a pause I said, "What fills my heart with joy is time to study. To reflect and learn from all that this sacred ground has taught me. And see where God leads after that."

"Then that's what you should do," she said.

That grief counselor was my Marie Kondo. Until that encounter, I had never felt permission to ask myself what idea of the future "sparked joy." And I had never felt the courage to let go of all the "have-tos" that spilled over into my life. That conversation changed my life and eventually led me to divinity school and a new chapter of growth and service for Donna and me in North Carolina.

Whatever our location or walk of life, we can take opportunities to declutter from the have-tos and create space for joy. What practices spark joy for you? For me, they include bird watching (Donna taught me); fishing (Spencer taught me); and visiting the Met Cloisters, an oasis of architectural beauty, art, and quiet located inside a busy New York City public park. They include canoeing on my favorite lake in the Adirondack Mountains as I seek out swimming holes and encounters with loons.

In Mississippi, singing in the gospel choir in our church rooted me in joy every week. Many of us find grace through music, and I am sure that choir singing kept me going through many times of difficulty. Watching the joy on the face of our choir director, singing, rocking, and clapping as one, melding my voice with those far stronger than mine, I felt caught up in some force of purpose far bigger than me. Over and over again, the Potter used that singing to put me back together again.

In ways unseen, often related only indirectly to the anxiety we are facing, when we put ourselves intentionally in spaces that spark joy, the Potter somehow declutters and renews us.

JOY-GROWING COMPANIONS

We need more than contemplative rhythms to get the love of God deep into our bones—we need people who do that for us. Joy is intrinsically relational and communal. According to missiologist Evelynne Reisacher, scientific studies show that joy is psychologically healthy and grows when spread from one person to another.[13]

During my years at Duke, Emmanuel Katongole and I shared an unlikely journey into a common mission. Catholic and Protestant. African and American. Him from a land colonized by the West. Me from a land that colonized. Him a happily single priest. Me a happily married man.

When we first started work on establishing the Center for Reconciliation at Duke Divinity School, we knew it would be a difficult task. We agreed that we might fail. But we made a vow: even if we failed, we would have fun along the way. We would keep pain and hope together.

One vision we carried forward was organizing a gathering of Christian leaders from countries in East Africa. We met in Kampala, Uganda.

The first day was very challenging, hearing all the painful stories of violence, church divisions, and political turmoil. That night, following our tradition, Emmanuel sat outside behind our guest house to debrief the day. We reflected on the stories of pain we heard. But for us, pain and hope were almost inseparable. Also following tradition, we spent a good deal of time laughing.

The next morning after the entire group worshiped together, we met in plenary, and invited the participants to stand and name gifts they had received so far during the gathering.

A participant from Rwanda stood up to share. Her name was Josephine Munyeli. Josephine was a survivor of the Rwandan genocide. In fact, her life was saved by a member of another ethnic group.

"I want to name the gift of the organizers of this gathering," said Josephine with a smile. "Last night I couldn't sleep because the organizers were laughing so loud outside my room!"

Emmanuel and I served side by side for almost ten years. Spread from one to the other, joy grew deep. It enabled us to stick with each other through thick and thin.

Joy-inspiring companionship has helped sustain people in most difficult places of suffering. In *Joy Unspeakable: Contemplative Practices of the Black Church*, Barbara A. Holmes writes of the deep wells of spirituality that rooted the activism of Fannie Lou Hamer of Mississippi. A sharecropping farmer, Hamer faced constant and brutal white oppression, including numerous beatings in jail.

Holmes tells of asking one of Hamer's friends why Hamer died so young. "Don't you get it?" said Hamer's friend. "If it hadn't been for the Civil Rights Movement, she would have died sooner." Writes Holmes, "It had never occurred to me that the Civil Rights Movement could become a monastic space, an opportunity for respite for a woman who had been 'buked and scorned' by the black-woman/man/children killing system of the day." Hamer, she continues, "entered the Civil Rights Movement as a novitiate enters a convent—not for retreat but for the restorative love of the community and the space to fight for justice."[14]

As with Fannie Lou Hamer, friendships in a common mission can root us in a joy that sustains us through thick and thin. I am afraid to think about who I would be without Spencer.

While our crisis almost ended our relationship, we had a joyous companionship on either side of that mess. We made each other better. We made each other laugh—constantly, until our sides ached. Spencer once told me, "I love you like a brother." Words like that will put the love of God into your bones. We need friends who do that for us. Who grow the joy within us, enabling us to continue to continue.

In our pandemic time, habits of isolation have increased, with more people working from home, no longer attending church in person, or seeking to protect themselves due to new fears and anxieties. In such a time, joy-growing companions are all the more important.

JOY OPENS US TO OTHERS

The British church leader and theologian Lesslie Newbigin spent his career serving alongside the people of India. Newbigin said that when our service in the world becomes mostly obedience to a command, "it misses the point. It tends to make mission a burden rather than a joy, to make it part of the law instead of part of the gospel." He reminds us that the Gospel of Luke testifies that after the resurrected Jesus was taken up into heaven, his disciples "worshiped him and returned to Jerusalem with great joy" (Luke 24:52). Newbigin declares good news: "Mission begins with an explosion of joy. The news that the rejected and crucified Jesus is alive is something that cannot possibly be suppressed."[15]

Joy cannot be suppressed. It will not stay contained in a cell of silence, the worship of a sanctuary, or the privacy of friendship. God's joy propels us out into the world in action and opens us to others.

We will wrestle with many pandemic-era challenges in this book, and we will see the deep change that is needed. The temptation with this new reality is to speed up our activism, to try harder and do more. But participating in God's deep change requires lives deeply rooted in joyful relationship. It is not becoming more active that makes us freer, it is becoming more beloved. It is getting more of God's explosive love into our bones. God's response to burnout is belovedness.

CHAPTER TWO

Centering the Vulnerable for a World of Rising Disparity

Truly He taught us to love one another
His law is love and His gospel is peace
Chains shall He break for the slave is our brother
And in His name all oppression shall cease . . .
Oh night divine
Oh night when Christ was born

"O HOLY NIGHT"

I love building outdoor fires, the slow way, with layers of paper, kindling, and logs, lighting a few places, and watching a tiny flame gradually become a blaze. I am a bit of a fire snob—I cringe when I see someone use lighter fluid, a casual squeeze followed by an eruption of fire. Lighter fluid is an accelerant. It greatly increases the speed of dynamics already present.

In many ways, the pandemic was an accelerant. It did not so much put society on a new highway but hit the gas pedal and hurtled us down roads we were already on. It amped up societal changes and realities already in motion.

The first eight weeks of the pandemic resulted in a decade's worth of e-commerce growth. Work went remote, lives moved online, and the default method for watching movies switched from theaters to online streaming. Prepandemic, many schools resisted remote learning, including my alma mater Duke Divinity School. But in 2021, after nearly one hundred years of offering a Master of Divinity, the school launched the degree in hybrid form. Before the pandemic how many of us worked remotely from home? Consulted a doctor online? Used online ordering and delivery as a default option for Christmas shopping? The pandemic accelerated the development of autonomous cars, and eventually an estimated one million lives per year will be saved from car accidents. We have sped far down these roads; they have introduced new normals, and there is no turning back.

It's true that some positive changes will come from the pandemic. But other changes are unacceptable: in America, as well as the rest of the world, the pandemic accelerated the disparity between haves and have-nots.

In the United States, there were record highs in both food lines and Wall Street stocks. While students at schools in high-poverty communities fell further behind and isolated with remote learning, enrollment in high-tuition private schools boomed, and many of these schools never stopped meeting in person. Demand for buying second homes doubled in 2020. At the same time, homelessness continues to grow, with nearly six hundred thousand people living without permanent homes or shelter, including over one hundred thousand children. While many small businesses were ruined, others prospered, especially giants such as Amazon, Facebook, Google, and Apple. Apple, which took over forty years to reach $1 trillion in value, doubled its value to $2 trillion in just twenty weeks in 2020 and then tripled its value by early 2022.

Globally, since anyone could catch Covid-19, many thought the pandemic would be the great equalizer. But as the pandemic

accelerated, so did historic highs of inequality between countries and between classes, with the world's richest 1 percent
gaining 27 percent of the world's income growth. Vaccine dis-
tribution has both illustrated and perpetuated this inequality:
the day I received my third vaccine in 2021, ninety percent of
Africans had received no vaccine.

Early twenty-first-century globalization showed us the
world was flat, leveling the playing field through technology
and the cyber world and making it as easy to develop and dis-
tribute a new product or service from Bengaluru (Bangalore)
as from Boston. But as the world became flat, humanity has
been dividing vertically.

GOD'S REVERSAL

The accelerating vertical divide between rich and poor is an
existential moral crisis facing America and the world. We know
this because of words preceding the birth of Jesus. Words of
praise and joy from Mary, they burst forth from this young
Jewish woman at the margins, soon to be the mother of God,
as she was greeted by her cousin Elizabeth:

> [The Lord] has shown strength with his arm;
>   he has scattered the proud in the thoughts of
>   their hearts;
> he has brought down the mighty from their thrones
>   and exalted those of humble estate;
> he has filled the hungry with good things,
>   and the rich he has sent away empty. (Luke 1:51-53)

In the arrival of Jesus, God turns the world upside down—
the proud, mighty, and rich are scattered, brought down, and
sent away empty, and the humble and hungry are exalted and

filled. This is good news! Mary's spirit "magnifies" and "rejoices in God [her] Savior" (Luke 1:46-47).

Mary's son is born, Jesus grows into adulthood, and he launches his public ministry with an inaugural address (Luke 4) in his hometown of Nazareth, declaring his mission statement to carry out God's great reversal:

> The Spirit of the Lord is on me,
>> because he has anointed me
>> to proclaim good news to the poor.
> He has sent me to proclaim freedom for the prisoners
>> and recovery of sight for the blind,
>> to set the oppressed free,
> to proclaim the year of the Lord's favor. (Luke 4:18-19 NIV)

Speaking words from Isaiah 61 here, Jesus sums up the non-negotiable ethical concern of God's special concern for the poor that runs throughout the Old Testament. Jesus says emphatically that God is antioppression. And antioppression toward what? Toward good news for the poor, the prisoners, the blind, and toward the "year of the Lord's favor," an Old Testament reference to the Jubilee year of liberation, of the setting free of prisoners and debts, and returning land to the original owners.

The vulnerable are at the center of God's action for the world in Jesus Christ. So, it is disturbing: this indisputable reality of our time, this vertical divide, this accelerating and alarming gap between haves and have-nots.

BECOMING NEIGHBOR

Later in Luke's Gospel, well into his ministry, Jesus tells a familiar story that helps us see more deeply into the vertical divides in our world. The story disturbed his listeners. Yet it lights up a pathway for renewal in our lives, communities, and churches, and as I mentioned in chapter one, it was central to my work with Spencer Perkins on racial justice and reconciliation.

The story is one of the most important Jesus ever told because it's his answer to the question, "How do I inherit eternal life?" A religious lawyer poses it to Jesus, and Jesus then asks him what the Bible says. "Love God, and love your neighbor as yourself," the lawyer answers. Jesus says he is correct. But the lawyer is not satisfied and asks a follow up question, "Who is my neighbor?"

Jesus answers by telling of a man walking the road to Jericho who is attacked, stripped, and left for dead by robbers. Two Jewish religious leaders pass by and see the victim, but do not stop to help. But a passing Samaritan stops, cares for the wounded man, and transports him to an inn on his donkey. Ending the story, Jesus asks, "Who was neighbor?" The lawyer answered, "The one who showed mercy." And Jesus says, "Go and do likewise." Note that Jesus changes the moral question, from the lawyer's "Who is my neighbor?" to "How do I become a neighbor?" (see Luke 10:25-37).

I'm sorry to upset popular Sunday school teaching, but this is not a tale of a kind person inspiring us to give to the needy. It's a story about being transformed in ways we often resist, a story that disturbed the lawyer and those listening.

Five actions of the Samaritan speak to five challenges in our new time of rising disparity. These actions show how we can be transformed from bystanders into neighbors.

THE FIRST CHALLENGE: CENTERING THE VULNERABLE

The first action of the Samaritan is allowing a vulnerable person to interrupt him, change the direction of his journey, and become central to his life. In contrast, like the two religious leaders who see the victim and ignore his plight, our societies are rapidly developing in ways that pass by those at the margins.

Consider one essential group of people without whom we could not have survived the pandemic: delivery workers. With the growth of e-commerce, they became indispensable to us, sometimes at risk to their own lives. But automation also sped up, driven by a need for contactless services. In China, for example, Alibaba (China's Amazon) began mass-producing delivery robots to replace delivery workers, bringing food and supplies to students on university campuses. In the United States, it is possible that by 2030 self-driving vehicles will replace bus, taxi, truck, and bike drivers. Drivers and delivery workers who were once indispensable will become disposable.

The grave danger is that vulnerable people will be considered more and more irrelevant. The richest 1 percent now own half the world's wealth, and the richest one hundred people own more than the poorest four billion. This century may create the most unequal societies in history.

According to Israeli historian Yuval Noah Harari, technological revolutions in bioengineering and artificial intelligence could push billions out of the job market while at the same time rapidly improving the lives of the elite. Harari writes that humanity could separate into "a small class of superhumans and a massive underclass" who are considered irrelevant:

> Once a real gap in ability opens between the rich and the poor, it will become almost impossible to close it. If the rich use their superior abilities to enrich themselves

further, and if more money can buy them enhanced bodies and brains, with time the gap will only widen. By 2100, the richest 1 percent might own not merely most of the world's wealth but also most of the world's beauty, creativity, and health.[1]

The poor may become what Harari calls a "useless class"—loved by their friends and family but useless from the viewpoint of the economic and political system. "Whereas in the past humanity had to struggle against exploitation," warns Harari, "in the twenty-first century the really big struggle will be against irrelevance."

How does the Samaritan's action speak to this danger? One day in 2021 in New York City, I passed lines and lines of people waiting for hours to receive a free rapid test for Covid-19. They were willing to wait because they put a high value on getting an immediate answer: "Am I infected?" A rapid test is not comprehensive. It doesn't tell us everything about our health. But as a reliable indicator of something important, it's extremely valuable.

More and more, these times in our world center the elite. With so much controversy about what real Christianity is, we need a rapid test to indicate whether we are practicing true religion or not.

In answering the lawyer with the story of the Samaritan who goes out of his way for the victim, Jesus provides us a twofold rapid test of whether Christian religion is true or false—true religion loves God and becomes neighbor to the vulnerable. If we are not allowing the vulnerable to interrupt our lives and change the direction of our churches, we have failed the rapid test.

THE SECOND CHALLENGE: CROSSING SOCIAL DIVIDES

The Samaritan's second action is helping the victim regardless of his religious and ethnic identity. He is willing to serve the vulnerable regardless of whether they are "my people."

According to biblical scholar Ken Bailey, this action was deeply disturbing to the lawyer and those listening. Bailey, who lived and taught in the Middle East for forty years, observed that the story is steeped in a culture in which a neighbor was "limited to the 'sons of your own people,'" to fellow Jews in their own family or town. In their eyes there was no obligation to help the victim.[2]

That Jesus chose a Samaritan as the model of mercy added to their outrage. Samaritans were a despised group, making the hero of the story not a good Jew but a repulsive outsider. In his journey into town seeking healing for the victim, the Samaritan had to engage the deep hostility between Jews and Samaritan because, as Bailey writes, a "Samaritan would not be safe in a Jewish town with a wounded [person] over the back of his riding animal."[3]

Here's the lesson: Jesus' story is about both unconditional action on behalf of any vulnerable person or group—whether we regard them as stranger, outsider, or despised "other"— who suffers injustice (the robbery and beating) and about conflict between mutually despising groups. It is both a "Just Samaritan" story about healing physical wounds, and a "Jewish-versus-Samaritan" story about healing social wounds.

During the pandemic it became clear that scientific and technical knowledge alone could not overcome the virus. As Harari wrote, "The biggest danger is not the virus itself. . . . The really big problem is our own inner demons, our own hatred, greed, and ignorance . . . blaming other countries, blaming ethnic and religious minorities."[4]

By taking the victim to a Jewish town, the Samaritan was entering unsettling territory and defying group loyalty. Many prejudices can stand in the way of engaging the vulnerable. Imagine the place that would be most unsettling for you to engage vulnerable people. A Bible study inside prison walls? A homeless settlement of people living in cars and tents? A rural town of mostly white Trump supporters devastated by opioid addiction? A black neighborhood suffering from gun violence? A community of many undocumented people, or refugees from a Muslim country?

One of the keenest Christian thinkers in our new pandemic era is Vinoth Ramachandra, a Sri Lankan who serves with the International Fellowship of Evangelical Students and holds a doctoral degree in nuclear engineering. Ramachandra says that more dangerous than any infectious disease over the long term are pandemics of fear:

> Science cannot provide the antidote to fear, although it can go a long way towards dispelling lies and misinformation. But it's "love that casts out fear" (John 4:18), the knowledge that we are loved unconditionally and that our worth as human beings does not rest on our color, gender, age, or achievements.[5]

The Samaritan is willing to serve the vulnerable regardless of who they are or whether they are "my people." Healing physical wounds requires engaging social wounds.

THE THIRD CHALLENGE: PAYING A HIGH COST

The Samaritan's third action is the high cost he pays to pursue healing for the victim. As Ken Bailey writes, the Samaritan "is using all his available resources (oil, wine, a cloth wrapping, riding animal, time, energy, and money) to care for the wounded man."[6] In addition, as a Samaritan transporting the man to an inn in Jewish territory, his actions are not only materially costly. He puts his own life at risk.

Here Jesus teaches that to become neighbor with the vulnerable requires costly and risky personal involvement. The effects of racism in America provide a lens to help us see what this looks like.

Jamaican sociologist Orlando Patterson of Harvard University contends that America has a paradoxical history of racist roots and resistance along with significant progress. After George Floyd's murder, Patterson pointed out that America was as racially segregated in 2020 as it was in the 1960s, the black poverty rate was two and a half times the white rate, the wealth gap was worsening, and more black children were growing up in high-poverty segregated areas than they did in 1970.[7]

In light of these facts, while Patterson saw "extraordinary progress in the changing attitudes of white Americans toward blacks and other minorities," he concluded that many whites "are not prepared to make the concessions that are important for the improvement of black lives."[8] *New York Times* columnist Charles Blow said it more bluntly during the protest marches after Floyd's murder: "Many white people have been moved by the current movement, but how will they respond when true equality threatens their privilege?"[9]

Those words make me flinch, remembering my arrival in Mississippi as a college student. I made a six-month commitment and then, captivated by the daily life of black people and white people living and serving together in a neighborhood at the margins, I stayed longer. I was excited.

But two years into my Mississippi journey, a racial crisis broke out that almost tore our church and ministry apart. Here's what bothered me: the black folks weren't talking about racism outside our church, but inside. My church. They were talking about me. They asked why whites were mostly in control. If we left everything "as is," they contended, whites would end up running everything. This I resisted. It challenged my identity of goodness and innocence. After all, I came to Mississippi to be part of the solution to poverty and racism. I was on the side of goodness.

It was a painful time. I almost left. But through an unexpected journey of pain, grace, and discovery, I came to see that the black people in our church were right. It was optional for me to deal with race. I could move to an all-white world, to an affluent all-white church, get distance from black folks, and not have to deal with race and inequality. I came to see that my black brothers and sisters didn't have that option. I came to understand my situation to be the power of privilege. Part of that privilege was living with blinders. Like the blinders on a horse, my privilege directed me only toward the reality I saw, while I remained unaware of and unbothered by the reality I didn't see. I didn't have to do anything to be caught up in this blindness—it was a kind of captivity.

Privilege is a form of power that blinds us to what is blindingly obvious for those who lack that privilege. And its hidden nature makes it dangerous. As Andy Crouch writes in his book *Playing God*, "Privilege is dangerous because of how easily it becomes invisible."[10] When we are blind to our privilege, we cannot see our neighbor or what it means to love that neighbor.

I had to confess that I was a big fan of justice for all—as long as it didn't threaten privilege for me. To stay in Mississippi meant beginning a painful change in my identity from solving to being saved.

The Samaritan used all the resources he had. Jesus' story tells us that healing the wounds of the vulnerable is costly. From the Samaritan, we learn that solidarity requires sacrifice.

THE FOURTH CHALLENGE: GETTING CLOSE TO THE PAIN

The Samaritan's fourth action is moving from distance to proximity with the victim. While two religious leaders keep away from the pain, he is willing to get close to pain and relationship with the vulnerable.

When Donna and I moved from Mississippi to North Carolina, we joined a church that was as strange for us as our interracial church in inner city Jackson had first been. The members of Blacknall Presbyterian Church in Durham were mostly white and well-off, including many affiliated with the elite Duke University. It was a time to learn about crossing divides from the other side of the tracks.

Eventually I was elected a church elder and asked to chair the Outreach Committee responsible for mission. The good news was that Blacknall was generous. While the average US congregation gives only 5 percent of its budget to domestic and international mission work, Blacknall gave over 20 percent, about $300,000 a year. But for me the challenging news was the name for this budget: "benevolence." We outsourced risk to others by sending funds to various faithful missionaries and ministries.

This benevolence model kept us distant from relationship with and learning from vulnerable people. The people and organizations we supported financially were in close relationship with pain—with communities racked by gun violence in Durham, with inmates in prisons, with children with disabilities, with people in Haiti. But for our own church members, the benevolence model often reduced us to bystanders.

Many ministries and organizations take a similar approach. I once read a popular book about Christian nonprofits and their achievements. It was filled with information about staffing, boards, fundraising, organizing methods, and programs. But strangely absent were the voices, lives, cultures, histories, and wisdom of the local people and places with which these ministries engage. In fact, the author called them "clients." Ministries and nonprofits put the lives of those they serve under intense scrutiny—whether a homeless woman seeking shelter for the night, or a Habitat for Humanity family proving they are in need and will be responsible, or a person addicted to drugs entering a rehabilitation program. But our ministries are diminished if they are only "clients."

The benevolence model comes with a benevolence identity. It's the corporate version of my mindset in Mississippi before our racial crisis. It asks for too little from us and our congregations —little time, little risk, little proximity with pain, little relationship with people across the divides of our city, little transformation. It blesses our lives as they are and blocks us from being changed by places and people who can teach us important truths—but only up close.

The Samaritan's action calls us to engage the vulnerable not from a distance—not as clients, but as up-close, face-to-face companions.

THE FIFTH CHALLENGE: BRINGING
CHANGE TO THE ROAD

Jesus' story of the robbers, the vulnerable victim, and the
boundary-crossing Samaritan invites us to imagine larger
forces at work on the Jericho Road. Here is the way Dr. Martin
Luther King Jr. put it in a 1967 speech:

> On the one hand we are called to play the good Samaritan
> on life's roadside; but that will be only an initial act. One
> day we must come to see that the whole Jericho road
> must be transformed so that men and women will not be
> constantly beaten and robbed as they make their journey
> on life's highway. True compassion is more than flinging
> a coin to a beggar; it is not haphazard and superficial. It
> comes to see that an edifice which produces beggars
> needs restructuring.[11]

Individual acts of mercy and justice alone cannot bring deep
physical and social healing. Here we meet a major obstacle
many American Christians face in becoming neighbor: to
transform the "whole Jericho road" regarding rising disparity
is impossible without thinking and working *institutionally*.

In recent years I've been haunted by the early deaths of a
number of black American men, friends who were part of our
church community in Mississippi. Most were in their forties,
the oldest was sixty-two. All died of "natural causes." Our
church was perhaps 150 members, half black and half white.
But I know of no similar deaths of any white members.

How could so many of our black men die so early? How can
this be "natural"? The disparity unmasked the consequences of
historic racial health care disparities, as seen in the disproportionate deaths of black Americans due to Covid-19.

Some dismiss talk of systemic racism as a form of cultural Marxism or secular religion. But church historian Mark Noll contends there is a tendency for American believers "to personalize and spiritualize the gospel to such an extent that the influence of world historical forces drops beneath the horizon of conscious thought."[12] Claims that life chances, good health, and social mobility are earned and deserved (or not) solely by individual effort don't hold up when we look at history.

Historical racism in America is like a malignant cancer—deeply rooted, capable of mutating into new forms, persistent, and infectious, with its consequences passed down generationally. As Orlando Patterson explains, the United States is "the only modern nation that had slavery in its midst from the very beginning," with inequality woven into political, economic, and judicial systems from slavery, and with state-supported segregation and violence—all of which have continuing harmful effects.[13] As just one example, federal housing policies beginning in the early 1940s excluded black people but allowed white people to buy houses at cheap rates, allowing white people to develop generational wealth.

In his 2019 book *The Color of Compromise*, public historian Jemar Tisby methodically lays out the case for the American church's complicity in the country's racist history and failure to fight against racism.

According to Tisby, one obstacle to a new future is that white evangelicals are unwilling to discuss systemic solutions, instead claiming that "structures and policies are not to blame," only "the harmful choices of individuals." Tisby says that while black Christians "tend to agree that a personal relationship with Jesus Christ is necessary for saving faith," at the same time "they also recognize that structures influence individuals and that addressing America's racial issues will require systemic change."[14]

Tisby believes both perspectives are needed to move toward a solution. "Every person makes choices and is accountable for the consequences. At the same time, injustice imposes limits on the opportunities and choices people have." We are all called to "analyze the larger patterns—ones that can operate independent of malicious intent—to see the historic and systemic picture and advocate for more effective solutions."[15]

Dr. King called us to see the "edifice" that hurts the most vulnerable and needs to be transformed. Human structures matter as well as human hearts. Addressing human structures delivers us from a narrow view of God's good news.

Jesus' story of the five actions of the Samaritan lights up a pathway to move from being bystanders to become neighbors: centering the vulnerable, crossing social divides, paying a high cost, getting close to the pain, and changing the road.

What are some ways to do this in our lives, communities, and churches? I will mention four meaningful ways to make Christian faith come alive as good news in this time of rising disparity.

PURSUE INCARNATIONAL KNOWLEDGE

As I've written about extensively, there is no hope without lament, and there is no reconciliation without lament.[16] But lament doesn't happen just anywhere or everywhere. In Scripture, lament cries out from vulnerable places where people experience and feel deep pain, oppression, and abandonment—Rachel, weeping in Ramah over her murdered child, who "refused to be consoled." Jeremiah feeling the "incurable wound" of the destruction of Judah. Jesus crying out from the Calvary cross, "My God, my God, why have you forsaken me?"

Lament is a heartfelt prayer and shout of protest from those who see, feel, and name the pain. In a word, lament is about being *bothered*. And only people who are deeply bothered have the passion needed to bring change. What if people do not see or feel the pain of disparity? What if they are not bothered by the way things are and remain safely distant from the vulnerable?

We faced this problem at Blacknall Presbyterian Church. The benevolence model not only kept us distant from the vulnerable, but also blocked us from lament. We were not deeply bothered.

With breaking news about every world crisis, we live with the illusion that we know what is going on. But internet information is not incarnational information. God created us with bodies, our bodies matter, and there are some things God can teach us only by relocating our bodies onto strange ground. Only by gaining incarnational knowledge face to face, body to body, can we become bothered.

At Blacknall, we learned this through the corporate practice of pilgrimage.

Our Blacknall pilgrimages focused on our home city of Durham and were done during the season of Lent. The goal was to join with Jesus in Gethsemane, praying "not my will but Thy will be done." Each pilgrimage was limited to twenty people who first met over several Sundays to discuss Durham's history of economics and race and the Bible's call to pilgrimage. That was followed by a weekend journey into Durham. There was both anticipation and trepidation; we were headed to places in our city that, for many of us, would feel like being in a difficult foreign country—just as strange, just as uncomfortable. Some confessed they'd rather build a house in Haiti than travel into unknown parts of Durham.

After a brief Friday night worship service, we carpooled across town from our familiar neighborhood to one of Durham's black communities and the home of Ann Atwater. Ann (who passed away in 2016) was a fearless advocate for poor people in Durham. Over dinner in her living room, she told stories about her rocky road to friendship with Ku Klux Klan activist C. P. Ellis in the 1970s (she almost stabbed him once) and their eventual attempt to improve public education (the 2019 movie *The Best of Enemies* tells their story). Before we left, Ann led us in singing her favorite hymn, "Just as I Am."[17]

On Saturday morning we drove into what police call Durham's "Bull's Eye" where most of the city's homicides happen. In a church basement we sang "Spirit of the Living God, Fall Afresh on Me," then heard stories of pain and hope from three men who had spent time in prison and were now serving the community. We met a mother who brought her teenage daughter's precious photo album, full of obituaries of friends who had been killed.

From there we drove to meet with members of Iglesia Emmanuel Church. While serving us lunch, several members told their immigration stories, walking across the desert from Mexico to Arizona.

Dinner was hosted by a black church just a few blocks from Blacknall, a very different neighborhood racially and economically. St. John's Baptist Church and Blacknall both had a one-hundred-year history, but those few blocks had kept us far apart. We spent the night with host families, then regathered Sunday morning for breakfast and the St. John's worship service.

Everywhere we went over those two days—Ann Atwater's house, the Bull's Eye, Iglesia Emmanuel, St. John's—were within a fifteen-minute drive of our church. Yet all were different worlds from ours. In our weeks of postpilgrimage reflection, we learned that some of us had never entered, eaten a meal, or stayed overnight in a black person's home. Others had never entered the Bull's Eye, met someone who had been in prison, worshiped in a black church, or been face-to-face with an immigrant from Mexico telling their story. One pilgrim said he would never look at the immigration question the same. In following years, the annual pilgrimage became even more powerful as a multiracial journey, with pilgrims from St. John's joining.

We saw more change in people over those three years of pilgrimage than any Bible study or sermon series held within the walls of our church could have delivered. It became a catalyst to move Blacknall beyond a benevolence vision of outreach.

Pilgrimage is not mission, such as building a Habitat house. It is not tourism, going somewhere to be entertained. Pilgrimage is a journey with companions onto strange and painful ground, seeking for it to become holy ground that changes us. Pilgrimage is grounded in the belief that God is already present in places of deep pain. There are some things God can teach us only through relocation—taking our bodies and our Bibles across divides with the vulnerable. Through pilgrimage, we who are not bothered can begin to get troubled.

ENTER CLOSE RELATIONSHIP WITH THE VULNERABLE

In *The Color of Compromise*, Jemar Tisby offers a critique of efforts to address America's racism solely through personal relationships across racial divides. And in an interview with *The*

Atlantic, Tisby said, "A mainly intrapersonal, friendship-based reconciliation [is] virtually powerless to change the structural and systemic inequalities along racial lines in this country."[18]

After a loud "Amen," I would add that as people who are built for relationship, we often find powerful connections between relational and structural transformation.

Take, for example, the stories of two of the most important leaders engaging America's criminal justice crisis: *Just Mercy* author Bryan Stevenson and Michelle Alexander, author of *The New Jim Crow*. Both Stevenson and Alexander are lawyers, and both tell the story of being blind to this crisis. But their lives were changed by unexpected encounters inside prison walls.

Stevenson grew up in the segregated South, graduated from Eastern University, and, as an afterthought, went to Harvard Law School. Disillusioned by classes that felt irrelevant, he interned in Atlanta with a center representing death row inmates across the South. His first prison visit was to meet a client named Henry. Stevenson started by apologizing, telling Henry that he was only a student and not a real lawyer yet. But Henry welcomed him, and they talked for three hours about family and life. Before Henry was returned roughly to his cell, he stood his ground and sang a hymn. That encounter, writes Stevenson, touched him with hope for human redemption and became a turning point in his life. Returning to Harvard, he plunged into learning about poverty, race, and the US judicial system. He went on to create the National Memorial for Peace and Justice in Alabama, the first center to memorialize the thousands of black people lynched by whites.[19]

What Michelle Alexander calls her awakening began with seeing the words "New Jim Crow" on a poster about mass incarceration in San Francisco. Thinking it was posted by some radical fringe group, Alexander quickly dismissed it, hopped on a bus, and headed to her new job with the ACLU's Racial Justice Project. But the years that followed, she says, changed her life:

> And it was really only through those years of representing victims of racial profiling and police brutality, and investigating patterns of drug law enforcement in poor communities of color, and attempting to assist people who had been released from prison as they faced just one unimaginable barrier after another . . . that I had my series of experiences that led to my own awakening that we hadn't ended racial caste in America.[20]

The deepest, long-term work for change comes not from people who are forced to change but who become persuaded and passionate for change, and central to that is life-changing relationship and encounter on strange and difficult ground.

As Alexander and Stevenson both experienced, we cannot learn about the vulnerable from a comfortable distance. Close relationship with vulnerable people can became a school of conversion in our lives, making us passionate advocates for change.

ENGAGE IN DEEP COMMON JOURNEYS

Another way to follow the Samaritan's footsteps is to invest significant resources in developing congregational and institutional initiatives that center on supporting and learning from what God is doing at the margins, and that go deep rather than wide. I call these Deep Common Journeys.

The year that Emmanuel Katongole and I cofounded the Duke Divinity School Center for Reconciliation, we went across the United States and world to learn what others were doing. One trip took us to Baltimore and the inner city community of Sandtown.

After a day walking the neighborhood, we were inspired by how New Song and New Born Ministries had interrupted the city's economic disparity and history of racial exclusion. In a fifteen-square-block area, 250 community residents had become Habitat for Humanity homeowners, an excellent charter school was serving 150 neighborhood children and placing graduates into colleges and universities, and arts and health care ministries were thriving along with an interracial church.

Part of our tour was led by a tall, gentle neighborhood leader named Elder Harris. Harris called himself a remainer, someone who chose to stay in Sandtown when most middle-class African Americans moved out. Right where we stood, on the ground of a former crack house and open-air drug market, Harris and his wife, Amelia, started Martha's Place, a beautifully renovated recovery home for addicted mothers. Behind the home was the Choose Life memorial garden with benches, trees, flowers, a mural, and a memorial to lives lost in the community to addiction and violence. "It does the spirit a lot of good to have beautiful spaces like this," Elder Harris said.

The tour finished, we stood on the street corner with Harris. I turned to him. "So Elder Harris," I said innocently, "what seminaries are sending their students to learn from what you all are doing here?"

There was a pregnant silence as Harris slowly turned to look at me. "*Seminaries?*" he said. "There ain't no *seminaries* sending students to Sandtown."

Harris floored me and humbled me. But on that street corner, the vision for the Teaching Communities program was born. Every summer in following years we sent Duke Divinity students to Sandtown for field education to learn from God's people who have not abandoned the margins of America. We also sent them to similar ministries in Phoenix, Chicago, and Mississippi.

Deep Common Journeys are initiatives that recognize, support, and develop companionships with the expertise God has placed in vulnerable communities. This same vision transformed Blacknall Presbyterian Church's approach to outreach.

The church pastors and elders united around moving from a model of benevolence to a model of discipleship, expressed as follows: "A Deep Common Journey is a partnership that we have entered into with a partner organization in mission. It expresses the hope that we would share together as a congregation in a transformative relationship in mission with our partners."[21]

We chose several ministries to invest in deeply and build mutual relationships with, including a university in the Democratic Republic of the Congo in East Africa led by Congolese, a temporary home to families with children in the crisis of homelessness in Durham, and a ministry in which children and adults with and without developmental disabilities experience belonging, kinship, and Christ's love. Deep Common Journeys move congregations from asking too little of their people with regard to the vulnerable, to taking great risks—and reaping the rewards.

CHAMPION INSTITUTIONAL AND POLICY CHANGE

Amazon founder Jeff Bezos didn't buy a mansion in Washington, DC, to enjoy the sweltering summers. He did it because it was strategic. To seek favorable political and economic policies, business and technology companies invest in lobbying each year as follows: Pharmaceutical and health industry, $5 billion. Insurance industry, $3 billion. Tech, $3 billion. Oil and gas, $2 billion.

What are we investing in protecting the most vulnerable? Writes Yuval Noah Harari,

> The economic system pressures me to expand and diversify my investment portfolio, but it gives me zero incentive to expand and diversify my compassion. So I strive to understand the mysteries of the stock exchange while making far less effort to understand the deep causes of suffering.[22]

Accelerating economic disparity, the effects of racism's history, the threat of hundreds of millions of people becoming a "useless" class—these are serious public matters. It is the church that is called to be a public voice for the Samaritan way in the arenas where political and economic policy is decided. Again, as Dr. King said of the Jericho Road, "True compassion is not haphazard and superficial. It comes to see that an edifice which produces beggars needs restructuring."[23]

New York Times columnist David Brooks is a Christian voice of reason in our contentious times. Wrestling with America's racial history, Brooks asserts that the way forward is through both reparations and integration, namely, "an official apology for centuries of slavery and discrimination, and spending money to reduce their effects."[24] Much of America's segregation is geographic, leading to long-suffering neighborhoods, and Brooks argues that lasting change must include giving reparations money to neighborhoods to support organizations led by experts who live there.

This will have a high cost because "racial disparity, reform [of] militaristic police departments and . . . an existential health crisis . . . is going to take government. It's going to take actual lawmaking, actual budgeting, complex compromises— all the boring, dogged work of government that is more C-SPAN than Instagram."[25]

Harari offers us a helpful guideline, recommending that "for every dollar and every minute we invest in improving artificial intelligence, it would be wise to invest a dollar and a minute in advancing human consciousness." To put that biblically, it would be faithful Christian discipleship to invest those dollars and minutes into designing and advancing public policies that address the racial and economic inequality in our country.

Evangelical church leader Rick Warren, Moral Monday movement leader Rev. William Barber, and Pope Francis disagree on many issues and doctrines. But Warren has gone before the US Senate to urge the church, public, and private sectors to collaborate to fight international poverty. Barber has led marches and protests to call attention to those being left behind in our time of rising disparity. And the pope has used his platform to call attention to the poorest of the poor across the world.

Pastor Rick, Pastor Barber, Your Holiness, may I propose a coalition of the willing? In our polarized time, we desperately need some common ground. One great cause that can unite us—from the Right, the Left, and in-between, evangelical, mainline, and Catholic—is to walk the Jericho Road together in the way of the Samaritan, together putting serving the vulnerable at the center of what it means to be a follower of Christ. Facing a future of "useless people," Christianity is being put to the test. For the sake of renewal in church and society, we must not pass by on the other side.

CHAPTER THREE

Being Peacemakers for a World of Surging Polarization

There is no way to peace along the way of safety. For peace must be dared. It is itself the great venture and can never be safe. Peace is the opposite of security. . . . Battles are won not with weapons, but with God. They are won when the way leads to the cross.

DIETRICH BONHOEFFER

Growing up in South Korea where my parents served as Presbyterian mission workers, I heard many stories about suffering during the three decades (1910–1945) that Japan colonized Korea.

Older Koreans told me about being forced to take Japanese names, learn the Japanese language, and worship at Shinto shrines; and they told me of Korean "comfort women" forced into the sexual service of Japanese soldiers. These injustices made me despise Japan.

Over seventeen years living in a black neighborhood in Mississippi, our interracial community and African American colleagues changed me deeply and led me into racial justice and reconciliation work. But well into middle age, my children would hear me privately mock Japan and Japanese people. "Dad, why do you dislike them so much?" they asked, and I was quick to explain.

In 2003 I was doing graduate studies at Duke Divinity School. One day in class I noticed a new student because he was Asian and, like me, was older. I thought he might be Korean, and I couldn't wait to introduce myself after class.

But my heart sank when the visitor told me who he was. He was a pastor from Japan, at Duke with his family for several months of sabbatical.

If this man had been Korean, I would have immediately invited him to my house for dinner with my family. But after five minutes I ended our conversation. I never offered to meet with him again. To be honest, I would have been just as likely to go to a heavy metal rock concert or ask for liver at Thanksgiving dinner. I had no desire to see him again, and I didn't give that Japanese pastor a second thought.

UNHEALED WRONGS

The pain inflicted on Korea by Japan brings to mind people who hurt us and never show remorse. I still find myself pushing them out of my mind as if I could bury them away. And as I remember my Korean friends, my pain doesn't come close to the trauma so many have experienced.

I think of my African American mentor John Perkins, who because of his civil rights work was ambushed in 1970 by Mississippi state police officers who beat and tortured him in a jail cell. These were government employees. But in more than fifty years since, not one of his persecutors was prosecuted or jailed for this crime. The state of Mississippi never offered a formal apology. Nor did any churches, although the officers were likely members somewhere.

Prejudices, blame, and bitter differences accelerated during the pandemic. An alarming number of Asian Americans were attacked and harassed with shouts of "Go back to your country!" The January 6, 2021, mob attack on the US Capitol removed the veil over resurgent racism as Confederate flags flew alongside "Jesus Saves" banners. From battles between Covid deniers and Covid absolutists, to dividing church denominations, to fierce battles over questions of sexuality and gender identity, disagreement moved to demonization and deep dislike.

In 2020 in Minneapolis, a police officer kept his knee on George Floyd's neck for almost nine minutes, murdering Floyd. Two other officers stood by and watched, failing to intervene. As author and Nobel Peace Prize recipient Elie Wiesel, a Holocaust survivor, once wrote, "We must take sides. *Neutrality* helps the oppressor, never the victim. *Silence* encourages the tormentor, never the tormented."[1]

I have friends in Hong Kong, Myanmar, and Ukraine, and it has been painful to watch their countries suffer from, respectively, suppression by mainland China, violent military rule, and Russian military invasion. You cannot make peace with someone who has a knee on your neck. Knees must come off necks.

Refusals to acknowledge wrong, to ask for forgiveness, to make repair, to take knees off necks—such refusals are obstacles to God's peace and reconciliation.

THE DANGER OF A SINGLE STORY

With unhealed wrongs and divides comes a danger. Nigerian novelist Chimamanda Ngozi Adichie called it the danger of a single story.

As Ngozi explained in a famous TED Talk, single stories reduce an entire group of people to one set of truths. "Show a people as one thing, only one thing, over and over again," she said, "and that is what they become." The problem is that "the single story creates stereotypes, and the problem with stereotypes is not that they are untrue, but that they are incomplete. They make one story become the whole story."[2]

From 2014 to 2019, I led six Mennonite Central Committee teams into North Korea while also working with South Koreans on the other side of the divided peninsula. Seventy years after the trauma of the Korean War, the mutual animosities still run deep. With no contact allowed between Koreans across the divide, the "one story" of wrongs committed by the other side easily becomes the whole story.

But I think of my Korean American mentor Rev. Syngman Rhee, who served a term as moderator of the Presbyterian Church USA. Syngman grew up in what is now North Korea, and his pastor-father was killed by North Korean Communists. Despite the wrong that he and others suffered, Syngman was one of the early pioneers to cross into North Korea to seek peace. He came back with more than the "single story" to tell of the North Korean people he met and became a leader in trying to heal the divide.

But Syngman was seen as a trespasser, called a traitor by many of his own people for going to North Korea. Here is how Syngman once put it to me: "To be a peacemaker is to be a bridge. And bridges get walked on from both sides."

To take sides, to not stand by when victims have a knee on their neck. To be a bridge between divided people, walked on from both sides. In this chapter we will see how both commitments are needed to heal wrongs and heal divides. It is, I believe, the "Christian difference" in a time of surging polarization—living into Jesus' words "Blessed are the peacemakers, for they shall be called children of God" (Matthew 5:9).

INVITING CONFLICT

From the United States to East Africa to Northeast Asia, I've been involved in many initiatives to repair social trauma and division. One lesson I've learned is that when wrongs or wounds are hidden or not admitted, they need to be brought into the open to be healed. At times this means allowing conflict to get worse before it can get better. And that is not safe. As Dietrich Bonhoeffer said, "peace is the opposite of security."

Hard questions make us feel uncomfortable. It was true for me when I heard this one: "Where do your churches stand on immigration?"

It was 2008, and the question was being pressed by Rev. Walter Contreras of the Evangelical Covenant Church. My colleague Emmanuel Katongole and I had organized a gathering at Duke Divinity School to discuss challenges and opportunities facing the ministry of reconciliation. About fifty US Christian leaders were present—pastors, scholars, authors, denominational leaders, grassroots activists, and nonprofit leaders.

We had many issues on the agenda. But Rev. Contreras was interested in only one thing. Again, he interrupted the program, "Where do your churches stand on immigration?" Now I was getting a little irritated.

Someone else in the room had heard enough. Rev. Harvey Clemons, a black pastor from Houston, stood up and turned to Contreras. "That is not an issue for my people," he said. "Black people have other problems which concern and affect us in this country."

The temperature in the room jumped. Hands shot up, asking to speak. We were about to break for lunch outside in Duke Gardens. Author Brenda Salter McNeil of Seattle Pacific

University proposed that those interested take up the immigration conversation there. It all made me a bit nervous.

A few minutes later when I arrived in the Gardens, I saw a stunning sight: about thirty people were gathered around an ornate fountain, including Walter Contreras and Harvey Clemons. There was debate, there was disagreement, but also some laughter. And there was intense listening.

Later that afternoon Rev. Clemons asked to speak. He said that for the first time his eyes were opened to see the connection between the work of his church in the Fifth Ward of Houston and the undocumented immigrants that were moving into adjacent communities.

"Earlier today I said this is not an issue for my people," he said. "Today my definition of 'my people' has been changed." The words of Leviticus 19:34, he said, had sprung to life for him: "The foreigner residing among you must be treated as your native-born. Love them as yourself, for you were foreigners in Egypt. I am the Lord your God" (NIV).

The next day we invited Rev. Clemons to give the message during the closing worship service. He preached about the "new *We*," which Jesus gives us in the new community of the church. And he left us with a disturbing question: Who is your *We*? When you say, "my people," who does that include, and who does that exclude?

Rev. Clemons had testified that his eyes were opened to people experiencing mistreatment of which he had not been aware. He also confessed he was blind and indifferent to this because they were not "his people." In other words, what is at stake in receiving a new *We* is both seeing and addressing wrongs and crossing a divide with strangers.

When we say "We," who do we mean? It's one of the most important questions pressing upon our lives in our polarized world.

WHO IS YOUR *WE*?

I love passports. I love their thickness, their look of authority. I love the access they bring. I have been privileged to travel many places, and each entry city has a stamp, from New Delhi to Kigali, Santiago to Seoul, Bucharest to Beirut, Cape Town to Chiang Mai.

Wrapped around my photo and name in my US passport is a bald eagle, grains of wheat, an American flag, and three big words: "We the People." That *We* has great power regarding my privilege in this world. "We the People of the United States." That *We* immediately shapes how I am seen by foreign eyes. It also marks who is in and who is out. When I lived in South Korea, I had to carry another identity card that named me like a quasi-extraterrestrial outsider: "Alien Registration Card." Korean people also have a strong sense of *We*-ness. I was an outsider, foreigner, alien, not Korean.

Our passports, birth certificates, and census data information are *We* markers that powerfully influence our identity, loyalty, privilege, and power. *Our* nation. *Our* family. *Our* cultural or ethnic group. Loving family, culture, language, and homeland in healthy ways rightly celebrates the beauty of human diversity. The boring sameness of the totalitarian world of George Orwell's *1984* novel is not the gospel world, which celebrates and respects difference. The gospel calls us to seek unity amid diversity and to resist uniformity or domination by the culture, ethnic group, or nation with the most power.

Yet our *We*'s can also disorder our loves and loyalties. They can limit and even twist us regarding who we do and don't befriend, debate issues with, and worship and read the Bible with. Whose welfare we favor and whose we neglect. What privilege and power we have and don't have, and who we share it with or keep it from. Our *We*'s can create borders that limit what wrongs and pain we see and address, and who we will allow to change us.

THE CHURCH'S PEACEMAKING DNA

Who are your people? Who is your *We*? Who is in and who is out?

As the book of Acts opens, these questions were on Jesus' mind in his final talk with his disciples. He has been killed on the cross and raised from the dead. He has spent forty days with his followers and is about to leave them.

His disciples ask him a final question: "Lord will you at this time restore the kingdom to Israel?" (Acts 1:6). Are you restoring the kingdom to *our* nation? To *our* people? The *We* of the disciples is limited to their Jewish peoplehood.

Jesus answers by naming their destiny, saying "you will receive power when the Holy Spirit has come upon you; and you will be my witnesses in Jerusalem, and in all Judea and Samaria, and to the end of the earth" (Acts 1:8). In Christian tradition, Jesus' "last words" are his seven sayings from the cross. Yet the resurrected Jesus gave these last words as well, and perhaps they are just as important. Outcast Samaritans and the ends of the earth were "them," not "us." They will be sent by the Holy Spirit on a journey to be bound to people who are not their people. Their *We* will be transformed.

After Jesus ascends to heaven, the journey begins after the disciples return to Jerusalem (Acts 2).

On the festival day of Pentecost, all in one room, the Holy Spirit suddenly interrupts them with strange power. Disruptive power. Not with a gentle breeze, but a violent wind. Not with soothing water but burning tongues of fire. This power puts strange languages upon their lips. They speak the languages of strangers and perhaps enemies. They are branded by the Spirit to be bound to people who are not their own.

Pentecost is the story of the birth of the church, marking its very DNA with building community and peace across differences and divides of ethnicity and language and social class. After Pentecost there is no more social life as usual. The Holy Spirit gives birth to a new community of peacemaking. A new *We*.

The new *We* expands rapidly after Pentecost. The disciples are swept across cultural barriers to heal an injustice between Greek- and Hebrew-speaking widows (Acts 6). They cross the barrier to outcast Samaritans (Acts 8). The disciple Peter is praying on a rooftop in the city of Joppa (Acts 10). Suddenly Roman soldiers arrive from Caesarea, sent from a military commander named Cornelius, asking Peter to come see him. But Peter resists. Romans were *them*, not us. Oppressors, not allies. Caesarea is enemy ground, not safe ground. Yet the Spirit tells Peter to get up and go with them because these strangers are sent from God (see Acts 10:19-20).

Peter goes to Caesarea. And in his encounter with Cornelius, he suddenly sees that the gospel is for Gentiles also. Peter welcomes his new Roman brothers to eat and stay with him. Crossing that boundary was not safe. But on the enemy ground of Caesarea, God expands Peter's *We*.

This is not the journey the disciples expected. They are taken to places and people they would never choose to go to if it were up to them to decide.

THE ANTIOCH MOMENT

Peacemaking across divides and injustices and swearing allegiance to a new Lord is a threat to those who prefer the way things are. When walls are seen as necessary or even sacred, border-crossing is trespassing. In Acts, as people join the new crosscultural community of the church, some are hunted down, attacked, and imprisoned, in efforts led by a fiery Jewish leader named Paul.

But in Damascus, on his way to persecute, Paul is dramatically converted to the way of Christ and is transformed into God's apostle of peace. Traveling to the city of Antioch, Paul starts the first truly multicultural, multiethnic church (Acts 11). Its members are Jew and Gentile, Roman and Greek, male and female. It is such a phenomenon that the citizens of Antioch do not know what to call them. So they invent a new name: "The disciples were called Christians first at Antioch" (Acts 11:26 NIV). From the beginning, peacemaking has been branded as Christian.

As Acts continues, Antioch makes headline news, so much so that Peter made a special trip from Jerusalem to see for himself. As told by Paul in Galatians (2:6-14), Peter got caught up in the excitement. But peace can be unpopular—it doesn't always do well at the polls. Some of Peter's associates followed him to Antioch. They were shocked to see him in the company of people who were not "our people." And Peter, the very one Jesus called "Rock," slid into the quicksand of superiority as he "began to draw back and separate himself from the Gentiles" (Galatians 2:12 NIV). Peter the Rock versus Paul the Reconciler—the showdown was set.

Paul could have let it go. He could have gone to Peter privately and, if I may paraphrase, reasoned like this: "My friend, maybe you're right. Sharing life across these divides is a mess.

Too awkward. Too much conflict. Let's just go back to our separate worlds and worship with our own. Once a year we'll have Martin Luther King Sunday, declare we're one in the Lord, sing kumbaya, and go back to our separate lives until next year."

But Paul didn't do that. He chose to escalate the conflict. He confronted Peter publicly, to his face. And here's why he chose that route: "I saw that they were not acting in line with the truth of the gospel" (Galatians 2:14 NIV). What is at stake in pursuing peace is not the least common denominator, not political correctness, not civility, not multiculturalism. What's at stake is the very truth of the gospel.

We have made too little of this epic Antioch moment. If Pentecost in Jerusalem marks the birth of the church, the controversial Jew-Gentile community in Antioch marks its graduation into adulthood. According to church historian Andrew Walls, the essence of Christianity is a crosscultural story, and it was the Gentile mission of the Antioch church that drove the gospel forward across cultural barriers.[3]

In the story from Pentecost to Antioch, who is the central actor? Not Peter, or Paul, or any disciple. God in the Holy Spirit is the central actor. Sending people into difficult terrain of righting wrongs and healing wounds is about God's choosing. We don't get to choose who "our people" are, who we make peace with, or what wrongs we address. God chooses. If Jesus was raised from the dead, there is no more social life as usual. At the center of God's action is peacemaking, creating a new *We* with strangers and enemies.

CHANGE THROUGH EMPATHETIC CONTACT

I love the apostle Peter because he is so passionate and so human. He fails, he begs forgiveness, he is full of bravado one moment and succumbs to weakness the next. His retreat from Gentile fellowship at Antioch reminds me of times I have resisted peace and a costly change in who my people are.

Ten years after my brief encounter with that Japanese pastor, I was serving as codirector of the Duke Center for Reconciliation. We had started a successful summer institute in the United States and another institute in East Africa, and had begun to explore Northeast Asia as a new place of partnership.

This meant I needed to travel to China and South Korea and, reluctantly, Japan. I didn't know anyone who could host me in Japan. But a Japanese composer named Yoko Sato had come to our Duke summer institute. I asked her for a recommendation. "I only know one person who might be a good host," she said. "He's a pastor in Tokyo." She said his name was Rev. Katsuki Hirano. "Oh, by the way, he did a sabbatical at Duke several years ago. Would you like me to introduce you?" I suddenly realized she was talking about the pastor I had spurned. This was a bit like Peter being summoned to Caesarea to meet Cornelius.

Well, I went to Japan. And Katsuki Hirano, the very man I brushed off at Duke, came all the way to the airport to greet me.

Over the next five days we traveled together to Tokyo and Nagasaki. Katsuki introduced me to Japanese culture and food. I met his colleagues, Christians living faithfully as a small minority, including Rev. Hiro Sekita, a leader in pursing legal justice for Koreans facing discrimination in Japan. In Nagasaki I stood with Katsuki in front of Urakami Cathedral where the US atomic bomb was dropped in 1945, killing seventy-five thousand civilians, including many of the Japanese Christians who lived in that area. Katsuki said many of those killed were ancestors of the "hidden Christians" in Nagasaki who kept the faith alive, underground, through 250 years of intense persecution. We walked together through the chilling Yasu-kuni Shrine in Tokyo, infamous for Koreans, which covers up Japanese war crimes and even "divinizes" leaders who led anti-Korean military campaigns.

Katsuki was often filled with shame. "We Japanese must apologize for many things," he said. I learned that Katsuki re-membered our five-minute encounter only too well. That filled *me* with shame. And while I had held tightly to a single story about Japanese people, he didn't do the same about Americans in spite of the bombings that killed hundreds of thousands of Japanese civilians.

I found myself being changed, and it was disturbing. How was this possible? How could I tell my Korean friends how much I loved my days in Japan? How much I learned from this wise, compassionate, and joyful man named Katsuki? When Katsuki came to my country I spent five minutes with him. But when I went to his country, he spent five days with me.

My encounter with Katsuki in Japan was the beginning of a journey of healing with Japanese people that expanded my *We*. Several years later, Katsuki returned to Duke for a second sab-batical. While he had arranged to stay in a hotel, Donna and I couldn't allow that. We welcomed him into our home for two months. And soon, Katsuki and I were traveling together to South Korea to give birth to the Christian Forum for Reconcili-ation in Northeast Asia, together with leaders from China, Hong Kong, Japan, and South Korea.

The historic suffering of Korean people at the hand of Japan formed me with a passion for justice. But as a single story, it also poisoned me. The one story I knew about Japan, how much Japan hurt Korea, was a true and ugly story. But it was my *only* story of Japan. Through the lens of that single story, I judged all Japanese people as not only guilty but undesirable.

Single stories are not untrue. They often carry unsettling truths that cannot be swept under a rug. They provide signposts that help us navigate a world of danger.

But single stories are incomplete. They can cause us to write off an entire group of people or reduce someone with whom we disagree to a simplistic label. Every one of us is touched by stories of conflict, bitterness, and division.

It is not easy to let go of our single stories. But looking back now, how happy I am that Katsuki interrupted my life. Our friendship and our common mission to address the wounds of Northeast Asia have made my pursuit of justice and peace truer and deeper. In every context of deep division and injustice, I am aware that where social change has happened, change through empathetic contact has been a critical element. The reunion of East and West Germany in 1990, the end of apartheid in South Africa in 1994, the peace accord in Northern Ireland in 1998—all were preceded by years of citizens crossing the divide at great risk and cost, forming coalitions to address wrongs and heal wounds.

When hostility is replaced with empathy and initiatives of repair are birthed, change through contact is an antidote to single stories.

PRACTICING RESTORATIVE JUSTICE

Polarized settings tend to be dominated by an either-or mindset. It's oppositional thinking. Either you are Right or Left, and ne'er the twain shall meet. They are too divided and opposed to coexist. We might think the same of a thumb and a forefinger. But the thumb is opposable—unlike other fingers it can be placed opposite fingers of the same hand (opposable thumbs are uncommon; be encouraged, the opossum has one too). Try to pick up a cup or use a pen without your thumb. But by holding thumb and forefinger together, well, miracles happen. When we hold two truths together in tension, the business field calls it "opposable thinking." This way of thinking can open higher levels of truth. We may think that we must choose between forgiveness and justice, that being merciful and being truthful are opposites. But the psalmist presents them as opposable: "Mercy and truth are met together; righteousness and peace have kissed each other" (Psalm 85:10 KJV). When seemingly opposed truths kiss, they open up greater truth.

The greater, opposable truth expressed in Psalm 85—holding truth with mercy, and justice with reconciliation—is the vision of restorative justice. In contrast to justice whose final end is to punish a wrong and compensate the victim, a restorative approach moves beyond to repair the relationship and build a new community. God is antioppression. Yet God's liberation is more than *anti* this or that. God's justice moves toward a goal, a new future, a positive new reality. It moves toward Psalm 85. It moves toward what Dr. King called "the beloved community."

"We must take sides," wrote Elie Wiesel. "*Neutrality* helps the oppressor, never the victim." That is about not sacrificing truth. "To be a peacemaker is to be a bridge," said Rev. Rhee. And as he said, "Bridges get walked on from both sides." That is about not sacrificing love. Taking sides against injustice or being bridges between divided groups—must we choose?

In the peacemaking journey of restorative justice that God invites us into, these callings are not opposed but, like the thumb and forefinger, opposable parts, which only by being held together can be faithful to the task.

Because love without truth lies. And truth without love kills.

LOVE WITHOUT TRUTH LIES

My friendship with Katsuki has not changed a critical truth: Japanese wrongs against Korean people still cry out for apology and repair from Japanese officials. The prophet Jeremiah railed against those crying "'peace, peace,' when there is no peace" (Jeremiah 6:14). Not being truthful about wrongs and wounds is false peace.

Paul's majestic passage about the ministry of reconciliation in 2 Corinthians 5 is preceded by the phrase "for Christ's love compels us" (2 Corinthians 5:14 NIV). At Antioch, Paul believed that Christ's love compelled him to confront Peter at Antioch because *the truth of the gospel was at stake.*

Paul offers us a guiding practice for peacemaking: *love without truth lies.*

Walter Contreras put that into practice at the 2012 gathering of US leaders at Duke. Contreras was troubled about the mistreatment of migrants and immigrants. Out of love and concern for them, he did not remain silent but repeatedly asked "Where do your churches stand on immigration?"

Harvey Clemons had the courage to seek truth as well, first by publicly disagreeing, and then by being willing to be changed. And as his *We* was expanded, Clemons was changed. When he returned to Houston, the new truth he learned led him to start an initiative of repair. His church began working with leading sociologists at Rice University to highlight immigration issues in Houston and beyond. Clemons and others started the Houston Immigration Coalition, a bipartisan initiative.

Without people who love us enough to us tell the truth, we cannot grow. And truthful peacemaking requires initiatives to repair what is unjust and what is broken. When we become part of a new *We,* we become a new person—a new me—who out of that personal change becomes an agent of change.

TRUTH WITHOUT LOVE KILLS

Love without truth lies. And truth without love kills.

Luke–Acts is a two-volume work, and we can sketch the contours of holistic peacemaking in Luke's story—from Jesus' mission statement to "proclaim good news to the poor" and "set the oppressed free" (Luke 4), to his Samaritan who pays a high cost to cross divides to serve the vulnerable (Luke 10), to his final words sending his disciples across borders and barriers to "the ends of the earth" with a new *We.*

This brings me, with fear and trembling, to perhaps the three most unpopular words Jesus ever said: "Love your enemies." They are also in Luke's story (6:27) and need to be added to Jesus' way of peacemaking, which Luke presents us. Those words disturbed his disciples. They certainly disturb me. But the new order of Jesus does not duplicate the old order of seeking change. It is a whole new reality. Jesus strikes at the roots of sin and violence.

Loving enemies doesn't mean ignoring injustice. Loving enemies does not minimize sin or evil. Loving those who hurt and offend and with whom we are in deep disagreement does not mean pretending everything is okay.

The love of Christ opposes oppression and abuse. And the love of Christ always seeks to engage and restore those caught in sin. On the night he was betrayed, Jesus washed the feet of Judas who would betray him and Peter who would deny him.

He washes the feet of those who oppose him not after they repent, but "while we were yet sinners" (Romans 5:8 KJV). In Christ, justice and liberation are not separated from love and reconciliation.

Spencer Perkins and I were very good at telling each other the truth. "You hurt me when you did this." "Well, you hurt me when you did that." "Yeah, that's because . . ." I cringe now, thinking about our letters to each other sharing our grievances. Years later I told a wise elder about that. He frowned, and said, "Never put something negative about someone else in writing. It has a way of becoming permanent." On and on it went, for months, trading truths about what was wrong about each other.

Truth without love began to kill our relationship, as well as our ability to persuade each other.

After we found our way to healing that I described in chapter one, a new phase of ministry opened. Spencer reflected deeply on the lessons from our breakthrough for addressing wounds and injustices. In the closing message at the last conference we organized, three days before his sudden death, Spencer shared one of his new convictions:

> What's so amazing about grace is that God forgives us and embraces us even though we don't deserve it. This means that if I know this loving God who is so full of grace, I will forgive, accept, and embrace those who, like me, don't deserve my grace and forgiveness. Our willingness and ability to give grace or to forgive others is an accurate indicator of how well we know God.[4]

Just as we cannot grow without people who tell us the truth and guide us on the road to repair what is wrong, we also need people who get this truth into our bones: even when we sin, we are beloved. Just as we need truthful peacemaking, we need loving peacemaking. Spencer's profound insight before his death was that holding onto grace does not diminish but strengthens the work of justice:

> Nothing—nothing—that I have been learning about grace diminishes my belief in Christians working for justice. . . . We must continue to speak on behalf of those who are oppressed. We must warn oppressors. But my willingness to forgive them is not dependent on how they respond. Being able to extend grace and to forgive people sets . . . us . . . free. . . . The ability to give grace while preaching justice—this will make our witness even more effective.[5]

The peacemaking way of Jesus holds together prophetic truth and pastoral love. It is a positive approach, always seeking restoration and healing. But it is also important to remember that we are not Jesus. We are not the Messiah. Unlike Jesus, we cannot, and sometimes must not, get close to every person who harms us. What God does call us to is seeking to forgive.

SOME PRACTICES TO HOLD TOGETHER TRUTH AND LOVE

Here are some actions we can take to put peacemaking into practice in our daily lives.

Raise uncomfortable questions. "Where are your churches on immigration?" Walter Contreras's question changed some life directions. Ask God for the courage to not fear conflict, and to speak up in your daily settings of work, school, worship. Do it with an eye not on self-interest, but on the vulnerable, the left out, the places of distrust and alienation. It's especially important to raise uncomfortable questions in our new era of information bubbles, where we spend too much time with people who think like we do.

Gain skills in peacemaking by getting closer to those who are different from you. Some people are better at telling the truth, others at being bridges. We need both in our lives in order to grow.

Put yourself on unfamiliar ground and seek connection with a group that you fear—and hope for "single stories" to be interrupted. A military general once told me that the greatest problem between North Korea and the United States was not military buildup but a lack of empathy. Our growing divisions in the United States and in the world are plagued with this problem. With others in your school, town, or church, agree to seek an opportunity to go onto unfamiliar ground. As the numbers of nonreligious and atheist students grew at Washington University in St. Louis, some Christians retreated. But students in the InterVarsity chapter on campus took a different approach. One day some of them went to meet atheists in the League of Freethinkers and asked if they would join in a weekend of community service in St. Louis. The atheists agreed. Serving together and informally sharing life experiences inspired mutual respect. A few weeks later, Freethinkers members approached the Christians and asked, "Can we do a Bible study together?"[6] For a congregation, organize a weekend pilgrimage of pain and hope into a community that you fear, seeking to listen and learn.

"But I say to you, love your enemies and pray for those who persecute you" (Matthew 5:44). Jesus said it clearly, directly. That person or group may be distant from you, in the pew or cubicle across the room, on your street, or even in the kitchen. We may not desire it, but Jesus instructed us to begin doing it, little by little. See what happens.

SCHOOLS OF CONVERSION, REPENTANCE, AND REPAIR

Another powerful peacemaking practice is creating schools of conversion across divides.

As I mentioned earlier, in 2011, my work with the Duke Center for Reconciliation brought me together with Katsuki and other Christian leaders in Asia to launch the Christian Forum for Reconciliation in Northeast Asia. Each year, leaders from China, Hong Kong, Japan, South Korea, Taiwan, and the United States meet in a different country in the region.

In 2015, fifty of us gathered in Nagasaki for six days— scholars, practitioners, pastors, and church leaders. We were women and men, younger and older, Protestant and Catholic. We went deep into the Bible. We worshiped together. We engaged difficult tensions and challenges. We ate together because eating together across divides is very important. As a Rwandan proverb says, "If you cannot hear the mouth eating you cannot hear the mouth crying."

With historic wounds and current tensions between their countries, this was as difficult for Northeast Asian leaders as is bringing together US Christian leaders in our polarization over politics and race. It was not an easy week.

One well-known Chinese leader had never been to Japan because of his bitter feelings toward Japan. During the week, I heard Japanese complain about the Koreans: "We can never satisfy them. How long must we wait to be forgiven?" A leader from China said in his country the 1945 atomic bomb on Nagasaki was good news: "That bomb liberated us from Japan. It was revenge for the Nanjing massacre." I heard Koreans complain about the Japanese: "They should be apologizing more."

The turning point of our Nagasaki Forum was our pilgrimage into the city to hear stories of pain and hope. We went to ground zero where the US atomic bomb exploded. We went to the site of Christian martyrs who were executed because they refused to obey the government.

Our final stop was a small museum. Going into the museum was risky. Through many photos and materials, it tells the story of Japanese military atrocities against Korea and China. We were surprised to learn that a Japanese pastor started the museum. And it was our Japanese leaders who insisted we go to the museum. Because they believed that love without truth is a lie.

When we arrived at the museum, I was nervous, wondering what was going to happen here.

Walking through the museum, we looked at the painful photographs of Korean women in sexual slavery. Massacres of Chinese. Japan's colonization of Korea.

As Chinese, Japanese, and Koreans walked side by side through the museum, something began to happen. I saw small groups talking together, reflecting, and telling their own stories. I saw tears. Shared tears.

When we were about to leave the museum, I saw Katsuki standing alone in a corner. He was shaking and crying with great emotion. A Korean leader named Jongho Kim, president of InterVarsity Korea, also saw Katsuki. Jongho went to Katsuki, embraced him and, with great emotion, said, "We must never let this happen again."

"We must never . . ." *We.* Not a Korean *We,* not a Japanese *We.* A new *We.* A *We* in which Christ is Lord. Where Christian peacemaking prevails over national and narrow interests.

Later, a Japanese professor said the museum changed her life. She saw a picture of a Korean woman in pain. "I have to wipe out her tears," she said. "Her tears became my tears." And her work of teaching and scholarship was never the same. That museum at the margins became a place of conversion.

We must never let this happen again. Forming these kinds of spaces is greatly needed in our increasingly polarized world. Places where, on uncommon ground, we interrupt single stories and together come to see a common truth that this pain here, and that injustice there, is unacceptable. Working and journeying together to take knees off necks. The ground where this happens is a ground of dying and being raised into new life. It is ground for becoming a new me. And that is where difficult and strange ground becomes holy ground.

CHAPTER FOUR

Redeeming Power for a World of Political Mediocrity

It is not true that a person of principle does not belong in politics; it is enough for his principles to be leavened with patience, deliberation, a sense of proportion, and an understanding of others. It is not true that only the unfeeling cynic, the vain, the brash and the vulgar can succeed in politics. It is true that such people are drawn to politics, but my experiences and observations confirm that politics as the practice of morality is possible.

VÁCLAV HAVEL, CZECH PLAYWRIGHT, FORMER DISSIDENT, AND FIRST PRESIDENT OF THE CZECH REPUBLIC

When a friend said someone in his church refused to receive Holy Communion during Sunday worship from a church elder who supported Donald Trump, it seemed to be a sign of a new strain of political cancer gripping the American church.

In 2020, *Christianity Today* asked readers, "When is it a sin to vote for a political candidate?" A few responses reveal our deep divides:

"I am part of a heavenly kingdom, not an earthly one. . . . I have never voted . . . [because] to vote is to place trust in government and human systems and not God."

"The Bible is extraordinarily clear on these matters. I believe it is a sin to vote for someone who will not protect the value of life.

Abortion is the watershed issue of our day, and if the church doesn't stand against it, we will usher in further judgment from God."

"King Jesus said his rule is good because it sets the oppressed free and proclaims justice for the poor. As we follow Jesus, that seems like it should be our priority."

"America's church-sanctioned sins of racism, xenophobia, homophobia, misogyny, and other inequities. . . . Voting not marked by repentance of these sins is doomed to perpetuate injustice and is therefore sinful."[1]

An integrated church used to be one in which diverse ethnic groups worshiped together. Now Christians of different political persuasions are segregating as if they worship different gods. We find ourselves overwhelmed by the "three Ps" of American politics in our time: polarization, paralysis, and pessimism.

Polarization. Battles over the presidency of Donald Trump, Covid-19, and race after the murder of George Floyd blew the lid off deep differences lurking in our hearts and minds. One nonpartisan survey showed that the United States is one of the most divided countries in the world, with 88 percent saying division accelerated during the pandemic. Almost 60 percent said people can't agree on basic facts, and 90 percent saw strong or very strong conflicts between supporters of different political parties.[2] Added to the mix are high levels of ethnic, racial, and religious conflict, creating a unique form of American toxicity and social exhaustion. No wonder 38 percent of pastors considered resigning during the pandemic.[3]

Paralysis. I have visited Haiti many times, and given the lack of roads, electricity, health care, and fair elections, I see why my friends there say the government has failed its people. But from political differences over election results, to the violent January 6, 2021, attack on the US Capitol, while the United States is no failed state, we do seem like a flailing state. The rapid development and mass production of a "made in America" vaccine within a year was a scientific turning point in human history. But one million Americans still died from the virus. Political gridlock exposed the limits of scientific and technological power. "There is no advanced industrial democracy in the world more politically divided, or politically dysfunctional, than the United States today," stated *Time* magazine in 2021.[4]

Pessimism. A young friend of mine told me he is fed up with the political choices of my generation and our lack of care for the future. As housing prices skyrocket, will he ever be able to own a home? Will Social Security exist when he gets older? Why are so many of our US Senators still white men with white hair? And because they did so little to stop climate change, what world will we, especially "the least of these," be living in fifty years from now? My friend is not alone. Commenting for CNN about young evangelicals who are denying their elders' politics, Kyle Meyaard-Schaap writes, "Because no political party can completely capture the fullness of the values [an evangelical] was taught, her community's embrace of partisan politics creates in her dissonance and disillusionment."[5]

Given these three Ps of American politics, no wonder that during the US 2020 election year—no matter your political views—all it took was opening social media for few seconds to get your blood boiling. Headed to Thanksgiving dinner after the contested November vote between Trump and Biden, many Americans vowed not to talk politics.

WHY THE CHURCH MUST TALK ABOUT POLITICS

At a family gathering, I'd probably recommend political quietism over a food fight with your uncle. But the political cancer that's afflicting the church will not be healed by being silent about politics. Because if the church is not talking about politics, it's not the church.

Politics is about power. And political power has enormous consequences—for good, for bad, for ugly. When something affects lives and makes our blood boil, rest assured: that's subject matter God watches closely and calls us to bring into the light.

Jesus was not a politician, and he rebuffed those who wanted a revolution against the Roman occupiers. But Jesus was not a political quietist. He talked a lot about power and why it matters. The church affirms this every time we recite the Apostles' Creed. The early church inserted only two people in the Creed—Jesus' mother and a politician—saying Jesus "was born of the virgin Mary [and] suffered under Pontius Pilate." Two of the disciples who Jesus chose for his close circle of twelve—Matthew the tax collector and collaborator with Rome, and Simon the revolutionary Zealot—were political enemies. Indeed, Jesus' final words to his disciples in the Bible are about power: "But you will receive power when the Holy Spirit comes upon you; and you will be my witnesses in Jerusalem and in all Judea and Samaria, and to the end of the earth" (Acts 1:8).

Jesus' life shows us that power matters, that power can cause suffering, and that power can be redeemed. Christ's love compels us to be fearless in talking about political power and the political challenges of our time.

From the United Nations to Washington, DC, to our state and city capitals, political decisions facing the new era in our world will be made with enormous consequences for years to come.

Political action is not of ultimate importance—God's kingdom and God's action is and, flowing from that, a church grounded in a community of character. But God created us with high responsibility as caretakers of this world, to choose life or death. And in this world, political power is both an indispensable good and an unparalleled danger. This is why political mediocrity is not an option, and why the church must actively nourish the good and vigilantly protect against danger.

THE INDISPENSABLE GOOD OF POLITICAL POWER

Understanding why political mediocrity is a threat begins with seeing how political power can be used for good. We can get a picture of that good by looking back at two of the most life-changing years in American political history.

Leading up to 1964, with others like her, a poor Mississippi sharecropper named Fannie Lou Hamer suffered brutal beatings trying to gain the right to vote for black people who simply wanted, in her words, "to live as decent human beings."[6] At the same time, in Washington, DC, President Lyndon Johnson led the drive for a historic Civil Rights Act to enforce voting rights and prohibit discrimination. Speaking for the bill, Johnson said,

> We have talked long enough in this country about equal rights. We have talked for one hundred years or more. It is time now to write the next chapter, and to write it in the books of law.[7]

Dr. Martin Luther King Jr. had lobbied hard for the bill. As he listened to Johnson's speech on TV, one close supporter said it was the only time he saw King cry.[8] But a white US senator from Georgia who opposed the bill, Herman Talmadge, felt very differently. Hearing the president's words, he said, made him feel: "Disappointed. Angry. Sick."[9]

Over just two years, President Johnson and the US Congress passed not only the Civil Rights Act but Medicaid, Medicare, Head Start, bills to fight poverty, the Voting Rights Act, and an immigration bill. "It was a decade of great strides toward social justice. Of hope," writes Johnson biographer Robert Caro. As each bill passed, some wept with joy, others were disappointed, angry, and sick. That is because, as Caro writes, "political power changes lives."[10]

Fannie Lou Hamer certainly agreed, casting her first vote that same year. Bill Pannell—who would later become a beloved professor and dean of the chapel at Fuller Seminary— was then a young black Youth for Christ evangelist from Detroit. In 1964, Pannell spoke at the World Congress for Evangelism in Berlin. Referencing the Civil Rights Act, he told the crowd, "Law did for me and my people in America what empty and high-powered evangelical preaching never did for a hundred years."[11]

Political power delivered a measure of social justice for marginalized Americans and for immigrants, for whom most white evangelical leaders not only refused to speak up at the time, but could not deliver even if they had preached otherwise. For while there are many things only the church can do to establish just relationships, the church cannot do what political power can do.

Here's another angle to view the massive impact of those two years and what the right use of political power can do. Historian Annette Gordon-Reed won a Pulitzer Prize for proving what many had previously denied—namely, that Thomas Jefferson fathered children with Sally Hemmings, the woman he enslaved. Gordon-Reed says that in bringing change, we need to take the long view: "There can be a tendency to say that [racism] is over. But you don't get rid of hundreds of years of slavery in a century. Blacks don't become full citizens until 1965. That is a blink of an eye in history."[12]

Historian Jon Meacham, author of a biography of Jefferson, echoes Gordon-Reed's conviction:

> The country we have right now . . . was really created in 1965. Not only with the Civil Rights Act and the Voting Rights Act but with the Immigration Naturalization Act, which totally changed the nature of the country. So no wonder this is so hard. No wonder we're having such a ferocious white reaction. . . . It's simply the lesson of history that we are in fact a better country than we were yesterday. It doesn't mean we're perfect. It doesn't mean we stop. But there are enough of us doing all we can as citizens and leaders to create a country that more of us can be proud of.[13]

Historically, the United States is a 250-year-old nation. But the America that seeks justice for all is only a 60-year-old nation. The political decisions made in 1964 and 1965 have shaped our daily lives in little ways we might not even think about. As Robert Caro writes:

> Every time a young man or woman goes to college on a federal education bill passed by Lyndon Johnson, that's

political power. Every time an elderly man or woman, or an impoverished man or woman of any age, gets a doctor's bill or a hospital bill and see that it's been paid by Medicare or Medicaid, that's political power. Every time a black man or woman is able to walk into a voting booth in the South because of Johnson's Voting Right Act, that's political power.[14]

Many of America's biggest technological breakthroughs sprang from private company and federal government cooperation—the internet, silicon chips, satellites, artificial limbs, flat screens, and even microwave ovens.[15] The government spent billions of dollars to develop a record-breaking vaccine and provided billions more in providing supplies and making advance purchases.

Having lived abroad many years, I find that Americans often take for granted what good government makes possible. I remember a Ugandan friend marveling as we watched a US president peacefully leaving office at the end of his term. In his country, President Museveni has been in office over thirty-five years, rigging elections to stay in power. I remember navigating potholes on Haitian roads at fifteen miles an hour; in fact, a friend there organizes church members to repair the dirt roads in their community. Recently on a call with a friend in the Democratic Republic of the Congo, his lights blinked. "Oh, that's the generator," he said. "We don't have electricity here." As a Texas Senator, Lyndon Johnson was beloved by the people of his state's Hill Country because his power brought them electricity for the first time.[16]

You and I can help an elderly stranger cross a river. But it takes political power to build a bridge. We can assist a person with a disability up the stairs of a subway station. It takes political power to install elevators across a city. A church can protest a war. It takes a president to sign a peace treaty. Churches can bring refugees into their homes who face religious and political persecution. But the new policies of the Immigration Act of 1965 literally transformed the face of America, bringing millions of people from Asia and Africa. The right and good use of political power made it possible. Not to mention electricity, getting potholes filled, and peaceful transfers of power.

THE UNPARALLELED DANGER OF POLITICAL POWER

The right use of political power can take strides that the church itself cannot replace and is indispensable for loving our neighbor. But political power also presents an unparalleled danger.

Of the war that President Johnson escalated, Robert Caro writes: "A young man—58,000 young men—dying a needless death in Vietnam. That's political power."[17] Caro also wrote a biography of perhaps the most powerful person in the history of New York City, Robert Moses, a public official who filled multiple offices over four decades. Caro calls Moses "the greatest builder in the history of America, perhaps in the history of world." Indeed, it's hard to cross a bridge in New York for which Moses was not responsible. Yet according to Caro, to build bridges and highways, Moses systematically displaced as many as five hundred thousand black, Hispanic, and poor white people, created slums, and divided up city residents by race and income. That's political power too.[18]

In 2018, a gunman entered a Pittsburgh synagogue during its morning worship service and killed eleven Jewish people. It was a horrifying crime. Add political power to anti-Semitism and it elevates evil into another dimension of destruction. The abuse of political power designed and carried out the Holocaust in Nazi Germany that killed six million Jews. Not to mention the evils of slavery in America, racial apartheid in South Africa, and genocide in Rwanda.

In each of these four contexts of pervasive political abuse, Christians were a majority and were mostly silent. Each place marks a failure of the church to exercise a prophetic voice and presence. Yet there were also Christian minorities who acted otherwise, embracing God's call to take up moral power to resist political abuse—antislavery campaigns in America, the Confessing Church in Germany, church-led anti-apartheid campaigns in South Africa, and Christians who protected people from ethnic groups being killed in Rwanda. In these four stories, we see both the excellence of the church with regard to political power, and our mediocrity.

Like proverbial oil and vinegar, here are the truths to shake together: Political power carries unparalleled danger. Political power is indispensable for human flourishing. The church cannot replace politics and political power. Politics cannot replace the church and its moral power. Political power can be morally ambiguous. Political power can be redeemed.

With this mix of truths in mind, let me offer a definition of politics that might help us see what's at stake: *The practice of politics is the use of political power for love of neighbor, just relationships, and the flourishing of life in common.*

If this is true, then disciples of Christ are called to embrace political complexity and learn the skills of appropriate political action. For the sake of loving our neighbor, just relationships, and the flourishing of life in common, we cannot afford political mediocrity.

Unfortunately, mediocrity is the current state of things. We see this in three contemporary problems: a weak understanding of how politics works, Christian captivity to political loyalties, and two flawed approaches to political engagement.

POLITICAL ILLITERACY

In seminary I learned a lot about prophets, both biblical and historical—from Jeremiah and Amos to Dorothy Day, Dietrich Bonhoeffer, and Desmond Tutu. But I don't remember studying any just politicians—not Josiah or Daniel in the Old Testament, not presidents Václav Havel or Nelson Mandela.

Our age elevates protest, outrage, disrupting the streets. But those sensibilities and skills are very different from those that achieve indispensable goods through political power. We often have a weak understanding of how politics works.

Our political education could begin with recovering stories like that of Barbara Jordan, the first African American elected to the Texas Senate after Reconstruction and the first Southern black woman elected to the US House of Representatives. One of my early political memories is hearing her majestic voice during the 1972 Watergate hearings as Congress debated the impeachment of President Richard Nixon. "My faith in the Constitution is whole; it is complete; it is total," said Jordan. "And I am not going to sit here and be an idle spectator to the diminution, the subversion, the destruction, of the Constitution."

Houston activist pastor Rev. Bill Lawson, who led boycotts in Jordan's hometown to desegregate city schools, knew Jordan well and described the difference between the prophetic and the political calling:

The civil rights movement brought to prominence a different sort of person than Barbara. The civil rights leaders were angry, passionate, impulsive people who drew attention to an ancient wrong in a dramatic way. In the language of the Olympics, they were the dash men; for the long haul you need distance runners. Barbara is a distance runner. It's simply not her style to get out with a sign, or to be disruptive. It is no accident that the impulsive and eloquent voices of the civil rights movement did not make the transition to positions of power and responsibility. Those sorts of positions belong to people like Barbara, people with a purpose but also with the ability to hold their own in political infighting with the establishment's best.[19]

In Jordan, we see what excellence in the nondramatic "distance runner" of political action requires, quite different from prophetic action.

Jordan deeply respected legislative bodies, studied Senate procedures, and became a legislative expert. She learned practical skills from fellow Texan Lyndon Johnson, developing a close political relationship with him. Of Johnson's political achievements, one commentator writes that Jordan admired "how much arm twisting and cajoling and convincing and political chips [Johnson] used up. But she also knew what they meant to real people."[20] She learned the skills required to get things done through alliances with people very different from her—skills of humor, of separating her ideology from political skill, of being unwilling to be typecast. She looked beyond immediate conflicts to making institutions work. She once wrote that "the Texas Senate was touted as the state's most exclusive club. To be effective I had to get inside the club, not just inside the chamber. I singled out the most influential and powerful members and determined to gain their respect." Needless to say, that was a club of mostly white men.[21]

Prophets don't join the club, they protest outside. Prophets critique institutions; a politician creates them. Prophetic excellence calls out right and wrong. Political excellence must calculate how to persuade voters and colleagues to get the right into law. Political literacy isn't found in the breaking news and talking heads of Fox and CNN, but C-SPAN's daily coverage of US government proceedings. A bit boring? Yes indeed.

Good politics is the art of the possible, a practical craft. By excelling in that craft, Jordan got things done that only politics can do: she helped set safety standards for blue-collar workers, expanded workers' compensation, and sponsored legislation that extended the Voting Rights Act to include Asian Americans, Hispanic Americans, and Native Americans.[22]

One of the key virtues of political excellence is a practice requiring patience, which has fallen into deep disfavor in our time: the art of *compromise*. When all issues are seen as a struggle of good versus evil, compromise is seen as a bargain with the devil. As David Brooks writes:

> The problem is that hyper-moralization destroys politics. Most of the time, politics is a battle between competing interests or an attempt to balance partial truths. But in this fervent state, it turns into a Manichean struggle of light and darkness. To compromise is to betray your very identity.[23]

Compromise can be a vice or a virtue. The book *The Color of Compromise* is a history of immoral concessions to white supremacy that contaminated Christian identity. But the give-and-take required to achieve political goods is a positive compromise that can be a sign of Christian maturity, rather than weakness. As British theologian J. I. Packer writes,

> The name given to the resolution of political conflict through debate is compromise. Whatever may be true in the field of ethics, compromise in politics means not the abandonment of principle, but realistic readiness to settle for what one thinks to be less than ideal when it is all that one can get at the moment. The principle that compromise expresses is that half a loaf is better than no bread.[24]

Protest and politics are not opposites. Yet holding them together requires the "opposable mind" discussed in chapter three—the thumb of resistance touching the forefinger of compromise. In our fervent state that Brooks calls hyper-moralization, our culture is far better at being thumbs. But as my Congolese friend Bungishabaku Katho has written in *Reading Jeremiah in Africa*, every nation needs prophets like Jeremiah, as well as politicians like Josiah.[25]

PARTYISM

Hoping "one of them" doesn't move in next door. Eliminating them from a job search. Having no close relationships with their kind. Being upset if your child married one. All this due to the person's political persuasion.

According to a study by Cass Sunstein, an American legal scholar and coauthor of the book *Nudge,* political discrimination has become so rampant that it is becoming a rival to racial discrimination. Sunstein calls the problem "partyism,"

whereby "some Republicans have an immediate aversive reaction to Democrats, and some Democrats have the same
aversive reaction to Republicans, so much so that they would
discriminate against them in hiring or promotion decisions, or
in imposing punishment."[26]

The story that begins this chapter—the church member re-
fusing Holy Communion from a Trump supporter—shows
how partyism pervades the church as well, segregating congregations by political views. Roy Lawson, an Independent
Christian Church minister who started preaching in the 1950s,
told *Christianity Today*, "The polarization is so deep now that
most churches lean to the Left or lean to the Right and they
think only left or right can be true Christians."[27] Polarization
turned to partyism veers toward idolatry. When asked if he is
a Democrat or a Republican, Pastor Eugene Cho says that his
response is, on what issue? "I don't believe that a party has a
monopoly on God's kingdom," he adds, "even though that's the
rhetoric that comes out from the left or the right."[28]

If we allow one party to be on God's side, we lose the moral
distance required to sort out propaganda from truth and to call
out that party's lies and abuses of power. One of the greatest
challenges to Christian discipleship today is political content
designed to inflame our worst passions. Cancel culture and
conspiracy culture are two sides of the same coin. As David
Brooks warns,

> When schools, community groups, and workplaces get de-
> fined by political membership, when speakers get disinvited
> from campus because they are beyond the pale, then every
> community gets dumber because they can't reap the ben-
> efits of diverging viewpoints and competing thought.[29]

Partyism breeds political mediocrity when government leaders automatically devalue proposals from and agreements with the opposing party. And it breeds spiritual mediocrity by replacing faith in God with faith in a political party or leader.

TWO FLAWED CHRISTIAN APPROACHES

The third problem of political mediocrity is the two dominant Christian approaches to political engagement—retreat and control.

We see these two approaches in the story church historian Brian Stanley tells in his book *Christianity in the Twentieth Century*. Writing of the failure of most Christian believers to speak up in Germany during the 1940's rise of Nazism and in Rwanda leading up to the 1994 genocide, the lesson for us, he says, is this: "Effective prophetic speech depends on a paradoxical balance between maintaining access to the sources of political power and preserving sufficient distance from those sources to enable moral independence to be safeguarded."[30]

Here is wisdom to guide our judgments about Christian life and political power. First, it clarifies the church's high calling regarding political power—namely, effective prophetic speech. Effective, that is, in seeing that political power is not abused but used for love of neighbor, just relationships, and the flourishing of life in common. Second, to live into that call, the church must do two things at the same time: both maintain access to and keep distance from political power.

Maintaining proper access and distance at the same time is a difficult task, with a great deal at stake. Like walking over a log across a raging river, it requires skill to sustain a "paradoxical balance," which, if we fail to do, will plummet us into danger.

Unfortunately, by making political power either peripheral or ultimate to our faith, many American congregations have fallen into one of two treacherous bodies of water that threaten to drown our witness and reputation. One is *political retreat*, the other *political control*.

The flawed approach of political retreat. *Retreat* is "an act or process of withdrawing especially from what is difficult, dangerous, or disagreeable."[31] As one person said in response to the question, "When is it a sin to vote for a political candidate?": "I am part of a heavenly kingdom, not an earthly one. . . . I have never voted . . . [because] to vote is to place trust in government and human systems and not God."[32]

Seeing politics as secular and not spiritual, the retreat approach locks politics with the dirty laundry in the closet to focus on personal devotion, evangelism, worship, and prayer. Fear of disunity is another reason for retreat from politics. By taking a "don't ask, don't tell" approach and keeping debate of political issues out of the pews, we may hope to avoid friction and controversy and protect the unity of the body.

But the danger of political retreat is heard in the voice of one Christian leader during the rise of the totalitarian National Socialist (or Nazi) movement in Germany: "National Socialism has kindly let us do as we like because we stay away from politics."[33] I witnessed this in South Korea, growing up there during years of rapid church growth. As long as Korean pastors and churches didn't criticize the dictatorship's abuses of power, they could grow their congregations as big as they wanted. The Christians who did otherwise lost seminary jobs, were persecuted and jailed, and sometimes even tortured and killed. What has Christianity become when we who prefer the social status quo make peace with political leaders who "kindly let us do as we like"—as long as we kindly let them do what they like?

For those tempted to retreat because they are rightly disillusioned about American politics today, I can only point you to what political retreat looks like from the bottom of the ladder of power. In his book *Reading While Black*, Wheaton College professor Esau McCaulley observes how many black Christians in America "have never had the luxury of separating our faith from political action."[34] In recent years, my friends in Hong Kong and Myanmar have suffered the sudden loss of their political and religious freedom. For them the cost is far higher to speak out against their government than it is for US citizens. Still, they have courageously done so, often in quiet yet subversive ways.

Eugene Cho said other pastors warned him to retreat from writing a book on politics. While admitting the tension of talking about controversial things today, Cho warns that "if we're not shaping and forming our congregations as imperfectly as we can as leaders, the reality is they are being discipled by someone else." It's far better, says Cho, that "our pastors, elders, deacons, and our thoughtful Christian leaders disciple our people around politics rather than cable news and political pundits."[35]

As history warns, when the church retreats from using its moral power to engage political power, it ceases to be the church.

The flawed approach of political control. The path of retreat flees from political power, seeing it as peripheral to Christian faith. But when political power becomes of ultimate importance it becomes an idol and the church loses its moral independence.

In his important 2010 book, *To Change the World*, sociologist James Davison Hunter showed how—from both the Left and the Right—the pursuit of and desire for political power and social control dominates American Christianity's approach to social change. In the partyism that is tearing apart both church and society, that seduction is living on steroids now.

As J. I. Packer explains, political control is seen in two extremes: the "politicized intentions of some Christian relativists [whose] goals reduce the Christian faith from a pilgrim path to heaven into a sociopolitical scheme for this present world" and the "political imperialism of some Christian biblicists who view the democratic power game as the modern equivalent of a holy war."[36]

One of the most dangerous forms this takes is seeking to create a Christian state in the image of a particular political leader or platform or understanding of Scripture. Christian nationalism is not only a US problem. David Swartz warns that it "pervades many global communities, sometimes with an intensity that surpasses churches in the US." He points to a survey of evangelicals at an international Lausanne Movement conference in which 58 percent of participants from the Global South agreed the Bible should be made the official law of the land in their country.[37]

Political illiteracy, partyism, and the flawed approaches of political retreat and political control—how can we address these challenges of political mediocrity? Given that political power is both an indispensable good and an unparalleled danger, what are the pathways toward redeeming political power?

I want to explore a positive approach for Christian political engagement through three avenues of action: living the alternative, being a prophetic voice with the vulnerable, and pursuing political love.

LIVE THE ALTERNATIVE

Bitter political differences between his twelve disciples and the options of retreat and control constantly pressed on Jesus.

In the political environment in which Jesus ministered, the Sadducees were upper-class religious leaders who sought political control by protecting the status quo and collaborating with the Roman rulers. Opposing them were the Zealots, who sought social control with plans of radical violence and revolution against Roman oppression. The Pharisees pursued power by purifying Jewish culture with right belief and keeping the letter of the law. And the Essenes retreated from politics and society to pursue spiritual disciplines.

But Jesus, and the early church after him, chose none of these options. Their political witness was grounded in an alternative—seeking to offer living proof that another life is possible in a world gripped by violence, division, and alienation from God.

Our politically polarized time cries out for such an alternative. Author and Anglican priest Tish Harrison Warren writes that she hears regularly from younger Christians "wondering aloud how the good news of Jesus can be true if the church is marred by racism, injustice, partisanship, and pettiness."[38] These signs of mediocrity add up to weak church life. Adding political power to such an ecclesial mix is hazardous.

My friend César García, a pastor from Colombia, is general secretary of the Mennonite World Conference. Out of the frustration of seeing political differences weaken and tear churches apart in his country, García wrote *What Is God's Kingdom and*

What Does Citizenship Look Like? Christian social witness, he writes, is grounded in "embodying a new social order in which relationships are equitable, economically balanced, and socially just." García calls this the centripetal force of God's power, that is, the way of Jesus first moving toward the center of the church itself. Out of the strength of an alternative community of character flows the church's centrifugal power, moving away from the center and outward into society to attract others.[39]

The quality of Christian political witness is grounded in the church's own repentance—identifying where, in these troubled times, we have failed to be a community of character, justice, and reconciliation, and being renewed in the way of Jesus. It is grounded in living an alternative.

Christian congregations, schools, and ministries that live the alternative face their brokenness before one another and before the love of God. They confront their sin and create structures of accountability and recovery. They grow in becoming multiethnic. They are communities where people openly, and even strongly, disagree—from politics to sexuality. But they disagree without dividing, continuing in relationships of commitment. Their ability to keep the lordship of Christ at the center enables them to critique every political party and leader, and every nation, where they fall short.

BE A PROPHETIC VOICE WITH THE VULNERABLE

Living the alternative gives us skills for walking the "moral independence" part of the paradoxical balance of Christian political witness. Yet skill in the right use of political power—the "accessing power" part of the balance—is just as critical.

Suffering from centuries of exploitation from politicians far and near, the Democratic Republic of the Congo is a country racked by injustice, violence, and poverty. Bungishabaku Katho left the country for doctoral studies in South Africa, focusing on the prophet Jeremiah. After finishing his PhD, he was offered a comfortable job there. But Jeremiah got deep into his bones. Katho returned to his home country, where he has become a rare blend of university teacher and scholar who meets with both rebel soldiers and government officials.

Katho tells how once King Zedekiah sent for Jeremiah from prison. Jeremiah asked the king, "Where are your prophets?" Indeed, the prophets had all fled because the national situation had become terrible. "But Jeremiah was present," says Katho. "He would not run away. He would not leave his nation." Katho continues:

> The prophets should be always there, and the church should always try to produce true prophets—those who will remind us of what God is saying about justice and fairness and the poor. All politicians and presidents should know that power is dangerous. They should know that if power if not guided by a prophetic voice, it is corrupted.[40]

Katho reports that many Congolese churches have become comfortable separating politics from faith. "Being comfortable is a danger for Christian faith," he warns. "It would be better to put ourselves in danger, in conflict with politicians. We are the majority in the Congo, yet the country is being destroyed. And I see that happening in America too."[41]

Unlike many other countries, US citizens have multiple channels to step out of our comfort zones and bring a moral voice on behalf of the vulnerable directly to political leaders at the city, state, and national levels. If you need guidance, consult one of the Christian agencies—from World Vision to MCC—that has advocacy offices in Washington, DC, and at the United Nations. Their very mission is to bring voices from the margins into halls of power.

PURSUE POLITICAL LOVE

Regarding accessing political power and the way of Jesus, the British pastor John Stott helps us sort out several key issues.

First, while in a narrow sense Jesus was not involved in politics, he was still seen as a threat by political authorities because of his very different view of power. As Stott explains,

> Although the teaching of Jesus was not overly political, it subverted unjust political structures, challenged oppression, and promised people that there was a new kingdom, characterized by justice, in which the truth rather than political promises set people free. The impact of this on social and political life was so profound that is quite legitimate to talk of "the politics of Jesus."[42]

Yet Jesus' politics was lived out in a very different context from our time. In the first-century birth of the church, Christians were a small group at the margins. So for example, while the apostles did not build hospitals, Christian hospitals are, writes Stott, "a legitimate extrapolation from Jesus' compassionate concern for the sick." We might say the same about the thousands of excellent faith-based agencies in the United States and world that seek to express Jesus' concern for the marginalized. According to this logic, asks Stott:

> Would [Jesus' disciples] have been politically active if they had had both the opportunity and the likelihood of success? I believe they would. For without appropriate

political action some social needs simply cannot be met. The apostles did not demand the abolition of slavery. But are we not glad and proud that nineteenth-century Christians did?[43]

Indeed, I think we are. To repeat Stott's key conclusion: without appropriate political action some social needs simply cannot be met. I would say it more strongly. The abolition of slavery did far more than meet "some social needs." It was an indispensable public good with enormous social consequences, the catalyst for a long journey toward dismantling oppression, which continues still. And it required political power. When political power is redeemed by skillfully navigating the paradoxical balance between access and distance, that power becomes one indispensable way of loving our neighbor.

And I dare say that when we do this well, we are practicing political love. Political love? I admit, in our partisan time, putting those words together sounds like a good opening for a comedy routine. But as I have tried to show, the right use of political power is indispensable for loving our neighbor. New language is itself a beginning point for redeeming power.

Dr. King expresses the essence of political love: "Power without love is reckless and abusive, and love without power is sentimental and anemic. Power at its best is love implementing the demands of justice, and justice at its best is power correcting everything that stands against love."[44]

Power is powerless without love, and love is powerless without power.

Living the alternative, prophetic advocacy with the vulnerable, political love—here are a few examples of how we practice these in our lives, communities, and churches.

Pray for political leaders. Prayer reminds us that ultimate power is in God's hands, not the world's. "Be still and know that I am God" (Psalm 46:10)—not the president you can't stand, not the pundit who makes your blood boil. And not us either.

Create and participate in "purple" spaces and friendships that blend "red" and "blue." One of the rarest things in America is an honest conversation across political divides, where people stay at the table and keep coming back. The call to sanctification, to Christlikeness, must burst that sanctimony. When I was in Durham, two of my fellow church members, both on the faculty at Duke University, strongly disagreed about politics. But they not only talked openly about their differences, they taught a course together and shared deep mutual affection. They made each other better. Purple friendships and spaces should not be rare for Christians. But like the cross-racial version, they require persistent intentionality. In annual Vermont town meetings, local citizens and legislators learn to disagree, compromise, and respect. Churches have much to learn from their centuries-long practices.[45]

Get involved in local politics. One purple space in Durham, North Carolina, is Durham CAN (Congregations, Associations, and Neighborhoods). Made up of hundreds of local citizens, Durham CAN spends months and months researching city issues, agreeing on a specific agenda (such as better afterschool programs, or street lighting in high-crime areas), and lobbying city government. *People of goodwill* is a Catholic term that Protestants (especially evangelicals) need to borrow. Since all people are created in the image of God, people of all faiths and of no faith are all capable of compassion, truth seeking, and justice. Connecting to people of goodwill opens us up to freshness and can create powerful coalitions of influence.

Put pressure on political power. The vulnerable suffer the most from political abuse and neglect. Whether local, national, or global, pick a place where that is happening, find a group that advocates to the political world, study their research on the issue, and support them with your time and money. Or find a church where you live that is connected to the vulnerable and put your support behind their advocacy to the political world. In an off-the-record meeting of nongovernmental organizations (NGOs) with a UN ambassador from one powerful country, he told us "Your letters matter. They cause me to pause, to reconsider. Keep sending them."

Elevate the political vocation. A president of a Christian university once told me that students want to serve with ministries like MCC, they want to go into activist work, but they don't want to go into politics. We have medical schools to train doctors, engineering schools to train builders, business schools to train entrepreneurs—but where are political leaders of character and moral vision formed? How many Christian schools, universities, and seminaries offer courses and formation programs? No wonder there is so much political mediocrity. Some are called to seek political influence by working within the political party they are in nearest agreement with. Indeed, I daresay more are called.

Czech president Václav Havel believed that politics as the practice of morality is possible. We see it in the political witness of Barbara Jordan. We see it in such leaders as Kim Dae-jung of South Korea, Nelson Mandela of South Africa, Anwar Sadat of Egypt, Yitzhak Rabin of Israel, and Ellen

Johnson Sirleaf of Liberia—all former presidents or prime ministers, and deserving winners of the Nobel Peace Prize.

But the moral vision of all these leaders carried a high cost—Mandela, Dae-jung, and Johnson Sirleaf were persecuted and jailed, Sadat and Rabin were assassinated by their own people for daring to walk toward a future of Arab–Israeli peace. The price they paid helps us remember that political power is both indispensable for good and an unparalleled danger. This is why political love, and our political discipleship, matters. Spiritual mediocrity is not an option for the church. And in this challenging new era in our world, neither is political mediocrity.

CHAPTER FIVE

Making Transnational Disciples for a World of American Blinders

*The question we are compelled to ask and answer by our lives is,
How might we show the love of God for all peoples,
a love that cannot be contained by any nation, a love that slices
through borders and boundaries and reaches into every
people group, every clan, every tribe, and every family?*

WILLIE JAMES JENNINGS, *ACTS: A THEOLOGICAL
COMMENTARY ON THE BIBLE*

People outside the United States know things most of us Americans are blind to, things we only learn on foreign soil.

A few things I've learned: Airport time doesn't have to be like waiting in a crowded dentist's office—at the Incheon International Airport near Seoul, a robot can escort you to your gate past live concerts, art activity centers, and vast indoor gardens. Many countries offer amazing, fresh, and fast street food—and cheaper than McDonald's chicken nuggets. In Thailand you can get pummeled in a traditional massage that will lift your body into a new dimension—$12 for two hours. And what the United States calls "soccer" the rest of the world calls "football"—a name they chose long before the NFL started and, for them, the truly beautiful game.

The pandemic opened American eyes to things we were blind to about the world.

Before 2020, most of us didn't even know what a pandemic was. But the pandemic touched every person on this planet. For the first time in the eight decades since World War II, we saw the entire world affected by the same devastating crisis at the same time.

We often hear that "global problems require global solutions." But, more accurately, the pandemic helped us see that there are border-crossing and border-creating problems that affect the whole world. For example, a virus starting in a market in Wuhan, China, leads to Asian Americans being shouted at and pushed to the ground on Manhattan streets. Pandemics are border-crossing and border-creating problems. So is climate change. Border-crossing problems are shared by all human beings and cannot be solved locally or nationally.

To faithfully engage these problems requires border-crossing people. Border-crossing problems require transnational solutions and transnational people.

The good news is, our Christian DNA is transnational. The cradle of Christianity is not a single city. It was not Jerusalem or modern-day Israel alone. As the book of Acts tells the story, Christianity's DNA was formed in a border-crossing journey in multiple cities, nations, languages, and political terrains— Jerusalem, Antioch, Athens, Rome, and Ethiopia (via the court official of the queen who met Philip, Acts 8:26-40). The DNA of Christianity is not only stamped multicultural and multiethnic, but multinational and multilingual.

Our future in this new time depends on living into that DNA, on becoming more joined to others, across national borders. But the challenge to become transnational disciples is this: our American eyes must be opened to many things we don't see.

THE TEAR GAS ENCOUNTER

When my parents served for sixteen years as Presbyterian mission workers in South Korea, one of their greatest challenges was learning things that mattered for Korean lives, to which, as Americans, they were blind.

When our family arrived in Seoul in 1966, Mom and Dad had never lived outside the United States. They spent their first two years in full-time study of the difficult language. (A fellow student famously said, "I studied Korean for two years. I learned a great deal during that time—including some Korean.") South Korea was a very different country then—impoverished and still recovering from the devastating Korean War (1950–1953), less than 5 percent Christian, and led by the authoritarian President Park Chung Hee, a military general who seized power through a coup d'état.

My parents' work followed many traditional missionary patterns—Bible studies with Korean university students who packed into Dad's upstairs study, Dad translating Christian literature, and Mom trudging to the margins to work with unwed mothers who faced social discrimination.

But their Christian identity was not prepared for another reality. Elections were controlled by the iron-fisted Park government, freedom of speech was restricted, martial law was sometimes imposed, and outspoken critics were often jailed and tortured. The 1970s were especially turbulent years.

Student demonstrations were so common, we became accustomed to the smell of police tear gas and the sight of troops in tanks parked at the gates of Yonsei University near our home.

One day after a Yonsei student "demo," Mom and Dad took a walk on campus. They saw a tear gas canister on the ground. On it were the words "Made in USA." My parents were from upstate New York upper-middle-class backgrounds, and they were certainly not raised as radicals. But seeing that tear gas canister was a turning point.

What did it mean to be missionaries from the United States, from the Presbyterian Church USA, when their government supported a regime that suppressed free speech and jailed and tortured and sometimes even killed its critics? When their country carried immense power on the Korean peninsula, including the fifty thousand US troops on over one hundred bases who were ubiquitous throughout the small country? Did Christian faith have anything to say about this?

Before the tear gas encounter, the powerful did not see my parents' Christian work as dangerous. But that changed, because border-crossing is viewed as trespassing by those who are threatened. The encounter opened my parents' eyes to see and meet Korean people they had not known before: Christians who were bravely speaking out in protest. The determined wives of jailed leaders who led passionate prayer meetings. Factory workers in dismal conditions, making inexpensive products for American companies to sell to American people.

Before the tear gas encounter, they did not know what those Koreans knew. They were blind to the impact of America on Korea. They did not know the world in which they lived.

WE DO NOT KNOW THE WORLD IN WHICH WE LIVE

In 1967, Dr. Martin Luther King Jr. also discovered that he had blinders.

That year King made a momentous decision, making opposition to the American war in Vietnam a central issue for his ministry. What followed was a speech in New York City titled "Beyond Vietnam: A Time to Break Silence." King connected the poor of the United States to the poor of Vietnam and examined the cost of the war to both. The nightmare King described was very different from his "I Have a Dream" speech. The war, he said, revealed the nation's soul to be "poisoned" by the "giant triplets of racism, materialism and militarism."[1]

Before this, King's *We* didn't include Vietnamese people. But the war transformed his understanding of loyalty. As King put it, Christ's disciples are given "loyalties which . . . go beyond our nation's self-defined goals and positions." Prioritizing an international issue was a paradigm shift for King. Many supporters begged him not to oppose the war, saying, in his words, "Peace and civil rights don't mix." In his speech, King replied, "They do not know the world in which they live."[2]

With those words, King defined the obstacle that my parents faced in Korea. An obstacle that also faces American believers in becoming border-crossing people. It is the problem of American blinders: We do not know the world in which we live.

The problem of American blinders is mirrored in the Mississippi story I told in chapter two, when a racial crisis almost tore our church apart. Before the crisis, I saw myself as being part of the solution to racial justice, on the side of goodness. But I came to see I had blinders on when it came to racism. I did not see the side of the country that my black brothers and sisters saw and experienced. I did not know the America in which I lived.

When a group of people are intimate with your power and its consequences in ways that are invisible to you, that is called privilege. As we saw in chapter two, privilege is a form of power that makes us blind to what is blindingly obvious to those who lack that privilege. Furthermore, its hidden nature makes it dangerous. As Andy Crouch writes in his book *Playing God*, "Privilege is dangerous because of how easily it becomes invisible."[3]

When we are blind to white privilege, it blinds us from seeing the pain of our neighbors in America who experience America differently. And when we are blind to American privilege, it prevents us from seeing our neighbor outside America and what it means to love that neighbor.

In a new pandemic era in which border-crossing problems are more prevalent than ever, American blinders pose three obstacles to becoming transnational disciples: might without sight, missing a bigger story about Christian faith, and a one-way traffic approach to mission.

MIGHT WITHOUT SIGHT

Blinders are a unique danger for American believers. In his book *The New Shape of World Christianity*, Mark Noll names several "chronic perils" facing American Christians in the world. One of those perils relates to power:

> However reluctant some Christian groups have been to talk directly about the exercise of power, power is a constant presence in the recent world history of Christianity —power as financial means, power as protected by

military might, power as dominance through communications media, power through control of education, and more. *No body of Christians has been as capable at exercising power as American believers, though few have been more reluctant to address questions of power face on.*[4]

The danger facing American believers in the world is not exercising power, but unexamined power. Power can be a gift. But only with eyes wide open. If we are blind to American might, that power can become dangerous. Unexamined power is the problem of might without sight.

One way this becomes a threat is when we do not see the influence of national American power on people outside America.

I have helped organize many peacemaking institutes in Northeast Asia and East Africa. The Asians and the Africans need no explanation why Americans are in the room. Indeed, they are far more familiar with the influence of US business, political, and church power on their countries than the American participants are. During the institutes, learning the history and stories—from the effect of US mining interests in the Congo to twenty-eight thousand US troops still stationed in South Korea—the blinders come off.

With my front-row seat at the United Nations in New York City, I see the power of the UN Security Council. Within the United Nations and its 193 member countries, the fifteen-member Security Council is the premiere global body for maintaining international peace and security. Its members can impose punishing sanctions, deploy UN troops, mandate cease fires, and take actions with binding power (yet only when the "Permanent Five" or "P5" members agree). In my position with MCC, I am part of a group of agencies that meets regularly with ambassadors on the Security Council. In the situations discussed in these off-the-record meetings, the United States is a powerful actor—Afghanistan (twenty-year US war), Democratic Republic of Congo (United States competing with China for its mineral wealth), the conflict between Palestinians and Israel (United States vetoes any Security Council action against Israel), Syria (US sanctions), the Korean peninsula (North and South Korea cannot sign a peace treaty without US support).

In all those countries, MCC has been deeply engaged with local partners for many years. As with my parents living in South Korea, we see the effects of US power up close—the good, the bad, and the ugly. Our long-term presence gives us eyes to see US power with foreign eyes.

Here is what is true about power, all at the same time. Power is dangerous. Power is a gift, if cautiously and tenderly embraced. Power is a demonic temptation. Power can be redeemed. Yet when power is redeemed, it is only with eyes wide open, in companionship with those who see what we do not see.

MISSING A BIGGER STORY ABOUT CHRISTIAN FAITH

Blinders also keep American believers from seeing a bigger story about who we are—our *transnational* story.

World Vision is one of the largest and most-respected NGOs in the world. But it has humble beginnings in 1950s Korea, during the trauma of the Korean War. American evangelist Bob Pierce was there. Moved by the suffering of Korean children and guided by his prayer, "Let my heart be broken by the things that break the heart of God," Pierce founded a ministry to serve them. His story as World Vision's founder is well known.

But scholar David Swartz stumbled on a different tale. To research World Vision's history for a book he was writing, Swartz went to Seoul. He met with a Korean leader at World Vision who told him that a man named Kyung-Chik Han was also a founder of World Vision. Trying to clarify, Swartz asked if he meant World Vision Korea. "No, the whole thing," the Korean replied.

On South Korean soil, Swartz learned a whole new story. Kyung-Chik Han was often called Pierce's "interpreter." But before Pierce came to Korea, Han was there: growing up in Pyongyang, studying at Princeton seminary, returning to Korea, pastoring the largest Presbyterian church in the world, using organizational genius to develop humanitarian networks and initiatives that would become the foundation of World Vision, and welcoming and working alongside Pierce.

The truth, writes Swartz, is that "Han discovered Pierce as much as Pierce discovered Han." Yet Swartz explains what happened next:

> Pierce became a legend, friend to presidents around the world and the recognized founder of World Vision. Han was ushered off the stage, disappearing from the American imagination. . . . But from Korea itself, there is another narrative, one that pushes back against a triumphalist American storyline and features Korean Christians influencing Americans.[5]

In his book *Facing West: American Evangelicals in an Age of World Christianity,* Swartz tells many other little-known stories about leaders from other countries reshaping American Christianity. For example, the Lausanne Movement founded by Billy Graham created a new platform for global evangelicals to cooperate on world mission. But the Westerners who led Lausanne at the time had a single-minded focus on evangelism and church planting. It was Latin American theologians like René Padilla and Samuel Escobar, who lived in contexts of violence and political abuse, who eventually persuaded Westerners such as John Stott that there should be no division between evangelism and social action.[6]

Being blind to transnational stories creates several obstacles to becoming border-crossing people.

First, many American believers imagine a single story of America as a nation that saves other nations. Transnational stories help us see that America is one nation among others, a nation with both gifts to offer and gaps that will be seen only through foreign eyes. Crosscultural specialist Adrian Pei speaks of a tendency for a "blind positivity" about America and American Christianity.[7] But Swartz explains that while Americans have "faced east," Christianity has been bidirectional, with global Christians "facing west" to correct and reshape American Christianity. American believers need foreign eyes to correct and enlarge our vision.

Second, transnational stories help us to see where American Christianity is captive to American culture. For my parents also, it was on foreign ground where they learned their Christianity was unmistakably American as well as Christian, and where their eyes were opened to the bigger story of who they were.

Third, transnational stories reveal the power of mutually transformative relationships. As much a problem as blind positivity about American believers is blind negativity, turning all missionaries into the tyrannical "Poisonwood Bible" Christians seen in the bestselling novel by Barbara Kingsolver.

Just as my parents were changed by Koreans for the better, the reverse was true. For many years, my mother worked in Seoul as a social worker at House of Grace, a home for unwed mothers whose children were often biracial, the offspring of American soldiers who abandoned them. Those mothers and their kids suffered severe discrimination in Korean society. It was American missionaries who saw that suffering and started House of Grace. House of Grace is today led by Koreans, and they have become leaders in addressing discrimination.

Being blind to transnational stories prevents us from receiving the gift of mutually transformative relationships. Today World Vision is one of the world's largest Christian organizations. And South Korea—a country of only 50 million— raises the second-largest amount of World Vision donations in the world, following only the United States. If that is a success story, the credit goes equally to Bob Pierce and Kyung-Chik Han.

ONE-WAY TRAFFIC

At the height of the pandemic in 2020, with unusual public honesty, UN Secretary-General António Guterres called for reform of the UN system, saying that, because of legacies of colonialism, "the nations that came out on top more than seven decades ago, have refused to contemplate the reforms needed to change power relations in international institutions."[8]

But it is not only the United Nations that needs a change in power relations—global Christian nonprofits do as well.

There's been much buzz in recent years about the decline of American Christianity in the United States and world. While it's true that the sending of missionaries from once-powerful US mainline denominations (Lutheran, Methodist, and Presbyterian) has receded throughout the world, the new face of US world missions is getting stronger via *global Christian nonprofits.*

The top twenty-five largest US charities include many Christian nonprofits working internationally. In 2021, six of those Christian nonprofits together received $6.6 billion dollars of income from US donors: Habitat for Humanity ($2.3 billion), World Vision ($1.2 billion from the United States alone), Compassion International ($1 billion), Samaritan's Purse ($900 million), MAP International ($600 million), and Cru ($600 million). Cru employs 25,000 Christian workers in 190 countries.[9] Of the thousands of NGOs in the world, World Vision is often considered one of the five largest, with 40,000 staff and income of almost $3 billion worldwide.[10]

The real story is not the *recession* of US global mission but the *replacement* of the mainline missionary-sending denominations by powerful, well-funded international Christian nonprofits that operate independently of denominations and are now major players in global humanitarianism. The new face of American global missions is led not by pastor-types but by CEO-types (one recent World Vision president, for example, had executive roles at Google, Motorola, Sky TV, and other digital businesses). An inside look is provided by *Beyond the Congregation: The World of Christian Nonprofits* by sociologist Christopher Scheitle, who examines nine areas of public impact—evangelism, publishing, relief and development, education and training, publishing and resources, radio and television, missions and missionary, fellowship and enrichment, advocacy and activism, and fundraising and grant making.

But most important is the organizational model driving all this. Unlike what he calls the "inefficient" nature of congregations, says Scheitle, when it comes to results, "the parachurch agency may be run like a business. . . . People who don't do the job can be dismissed. Decisions can be quickly made. Their promotions are slick and results obvious. Pragmatic people like this." This "highly rationalized business model," he says, "allows parachurch organizations to produce more goods and services faster, more efficiently, and more predictably." Scheitle celebrates what he calls the "bureaucratic model" that drives global Christian nonprofits.[11]

But to assume that the "bigger is better" American business model of global mission is a great good is to be blind to the effects of unexamined power.

A different lens for evaluating large US Christian nonprofits is provided by Andy Crouch in *Playing God*. Their unexamined power is not a danger of the "the ill-intentioned, but the well-intentioned," and this unprecedented global power has "classic qualities of divinity": *Omnipresence*—simultaneously present in dozens and dozens of countries at once. *Omniscience*—knowing a great deal about the beneficiaries, with very little revealed from the benefactors. *Omnipotence*—able to work with extreme efficiency and productivity because of technology. Global Christian nonprofits, he says, have become "one of the great benevolent god-playing enterprises of our time." But God's work is inhibited when financial resources are used "with such force, and with so little real trust building or relationship, that we maintain a safe distance between ourselves and the recipients of our largesse." Tragically, "charity becomes a matter of marketing, simply persuading the powerful to use their godlike powers for good."[12]

The bureaucratic model of mission is one of one-way traffic—giving and sending—not of relationship between equals and friends. *How* we do mission matters as much as *what* we do.

BECOMING TRANSNATIONAL DISCIPLES

The road to becoming transnational disciples is not one-way but two-way. Again remembering Dr. King's words, transnational disciples form "loyalties which . . . go beyond our nation's self-defined goals and positions."[13]

The Apostles' Creed testifies that Christians believe in "one holy, catholic church"—that's a small-*c* catholic, the church universal, the one body of Christ made up of people of all nations and cultures. The pandemic itself revealed the truth about our transnational identity. As Stanley Hauerwas put it:

> The pandemic reveals that we're a catholic people. That we are bound to one another around the world in a way that how Christians fare in China makes a good deal of difference for how we fare in North Carolina. And that we are joined in a common life that gives us a sense of obligation to one another. That doesn't mean that we are not also bound to those who do not claim to be Christian. We are all creatures of a good God.[14]

One pathway for American believers to become transnational disciples is to move from one-way practices of sending and giving to two-way practices of sharing and receiving. Following are three two-way practices for our lives, communities, and churches.

EXPAND WHO YOU READ

When did you last read a blog or book by a Christian from the Majority World?

Although Christianity's growth has shifted from North to South, many key Majority World voices are overlooked because they lack a major publishing platform. When our Christian reading and publishing is largely American- and Western-centric, we are deprived of many important truths.

Thankfully groups like Langham Publishing (funded by John Stott's royalties) are trying to change that. Congolese Christians have much to teach us about living in times of turbulence; Langham published Bungishabaku Katho's *Reading Jeremiah in Africa: Biblical Essays in Sociopolitical Imagination.* Jeremiah comes alive through Katho, as readers learn how studying the prophet changed his life, sending him back to his home to engage challenges of war, violence, and ethnic conflict in both church and society.

Read the blog of Vinoth Ramachandra of Sri Lanka, who works with the International Fellowship of Evangelical Students. Read the writings of Ruth Padilla DeBorst in Costa Rica, Paulus Widjaja of Indonesia, and César García of Colombia. My friend and Notre Dame scholar Emmanuel Katongole spends several months every year in his native Uganda and is giving leading thought to issues of climate crisis.[15]

To become transnational disciples, our one-way reading needs to become two-way. The Bible takes on fresh meaning when we read it through foreign eyes.

MAKE MAJORITY WORLD LEADERS EQUAL AND EMPOWERED

The face of Christianity's growth is shifting globally. But in US-based global Christian nonprofits, who leads and who decides remains largely in the hands of white Americans.

In my eight years of MCC service in Asia and engaging the United Nations in New York City, I've been in many international meetings with leaders and staff from other ministries and NGOs. The rooms are still dominated by white Westerners.

This suggests the same is true of the rooms where their executive teams and board members meet.[16]

In his book *Reconciliation Blues: A Black Evangelical's Inside View of White Christianity*, Ed Gilbreath helps remove our blinders, revealing the obstacles and discontent facing minority groups working inside of Christian organizations in the United States. But while there has been more focus on making our Christian nonprofits in the US multiethnic, there are still very few US ethnic minorities and non-Americans in leadership positions in international agencies.

A two-way approach calls us to lean into what Adrian Pei says about his many years with the Epic Movement, the Asian American ministry of Cru. He constantly veered between "Do I assimilate, or do I disengage?" His "Six Postures of Ethnic Minority Culture Towards Majority Culture" are revealing: unaware, angry and wounded, silent and resigned, duty and pleasing, unity as assimilation. The sixth posture is the goal: being equal and empowered. "This means we see ourselves as equally valuable as whites, and as a result built crosscultural partnerships for both sides' benefit. We take the initiative out of the beauty of how God created us, rather than out of reaction to how others define us."[17]

Paul Tokunaga, who served many years with InterVarsity Christian Fellowship, proposed an initiative to build up minority leaders within InterVarsity to lead at the highest levels. Called the Daniel Project, each leader was assigned a mentor for at least a year (the mentors were paid). After the program's first year, twelve of the fourteen participants were promoted, and in 2016 InterVarsity selected its first nonwhite president in its seventy-five-year history: Taiwanese American Tom Lin. Tokunaga—who served over thirty years with InterVarsity—testifies that it took many years to build up the trust and will to make these changes.[18]

Making minorities equal and empowered requires tireless intentionality.

PURSUE TRANSNATIONAL FRIENDSHIP IN COMMON MISSION

The one-way traffic model of mission isn't a relationship of equals, and it doesn't have the power to remove blinders in order to see unexamined power. But there is an alternative: lifetime crosscultural friendships of mutuality. According to missiologist Dana Robert:

> For unknown numbers of missionaries and indigenous Christian leaders in the early to mid-twentieth century, friendship was a potent yet under-recognized ethic and practice in the creation of world Christianity as a multi-cultural community. Indeed, without friendship as clear witness to Christlike love, the inequities and racism of the colonial period might have prevented the spread of Christianity across cultures.[19]

Authentic crosscultural friendships are costly. They require a commitment to specific people from other cultures, learning the language and ways of the local context, developing reciprocal relationships, and joining in common mission.[20] They last long enough for the blinders to come off, and a willingness to go where new revelations lead.

My parents' encounter with the tear gas canister in Seoul launched a journey into lifetime crosscultural friendship.

They soon met other concerned missionaries who began meeting every week in a "Monday Night Group." Many a week

I came home from school to twenty pairs of shoes at the door, Korean-style, passing through our living room full of Protestant and Catholic missionaries from the United States, Canada, and Europe. They sought out US members of Congress visiting South Korea. Went into dimly lit factories to evaluate the eyesight of workers. Brought critical information in to Koreans whose media was censored. Took information out to foreign media about the suffering inside. Brought clothing and care to jailed pastors and professors.

Once Mom and Dad hid a Korean couple in our home who were wanted by the police. Another time, eight Korean labor organizers were falsely accused of being communist sympathizers and sentenced to death without a trial. My mother was part of the tumultuous aftermath, when wives of men who were to be hung to death the next day cried out in protest while being violently pulled by police. A few days later my father and several colleagues went to the front of the US embassy in downtown Seoul, donned hoods and nooses, and led a prayer vigil holding banners that said, "Must the US support oppression of human rights?" and "Is this nothing to you?" Later that day South Korean intelligence officers came to our home, took Dad downtown, and questioned him for several hours.[21]

My parents took their new story back to the United States. When the wives of jailed Korean activists began knitting purple shawls as symbols of hope, Mom carried bundles of them on the plane to sell at churches, using the funds to support the women. "Sold in USA" purple shawls became a response to "Made in USA" tear gas canisters.

Those shawls helped take blinders off American believers to see not only how their country's power affected others, but how they were not powerless to respond. Korean Christians opened my parents' American eyes to a deeper gospel. My parents opened Korean eyes wider too.

The border-crossing problems of our world require border-crossing solutions, and border-crossing solutions require border-crossing disciples. At the end of the day, it's not about making Americans more Christian but Christians less American.

CHAPTER SIX

Pursuing Private Integrity for a World of Public Validation

How can you draw close to God when you are far from your own self?

AUGUSTINE, *CONFESSIONS*

In March 2020 Donna and I were visiting friends in Mississippi when it became clear that Covid was a crisis. We decided Donna would return to New York City and I would fly directly to Vermont to help support my eighty-seven-year-old father.

Soon Donna was on the frontlines as a nurse. With my work representing MCC at the United Nations, serious global challenges emerged from many angles. I was immersed in online international conference calls with colleagues across the world.

But after a couple weeks of full-time online work and monastic isolation in small-town Vermont with Dad—moving between my computer screen and outside to the backyard—I began to feel inner turbulence. Instead of a UN office director meeting with ambassadors, UN staff, and NGO colleagues amid New York's bustling streets, I was feeling more like Dr. Doolittle, surrounded by woodpeckers, wild turkeys, and the two chipmunks raiding the bird feeder.

On the church feast day of Annunciation, I opened my daily devotional book to the story of Mary's encounter with the angel Gabriel. The angel tells Mary she will give birth to the Son of God Most High. Mary responds, "Let it be to me according to your word."

In this moment of global crisis, what was God's word to me? Sitting there surrounded by quiet, to what special call, great task, world-changing work was I to give the answer, "Let it be to me"?

As I waited for an answer, the disruption of the pandemic blew open the closet of my heart, and things began creeping out.

My recent five years with Donna living in South Korea and working in Northeast Asia had been full of rewarding and meaningful work. But, from deep inside me, unwelcome feelings emerged of regret, loss, and grief from difficulties in my family and marriage over those same years.

The distance from our three children had been hard on our relationships with them. While we were across an ocean, each of them had experienced some very difficult times, and we hadn't been there to walk beside them.

My mother had passed away after a rapid six-month decline. I'm so grateful we got back to the United States to be at her bedside during her final days. But after she died, unhealed wounds from the past emerged with my siblings.

In Korea, Donna and I shared the same leadership job, working with our desks a few feet apart. For us at least, it wasn't a recipe for romance. She attends to every incoming email while I plot plans to save the world. Donna has an open-door policy. I am fully available to anyone. Anywhere. For fifteen minutes. She is the engineer, I the poet. In an abstract painting, where Donna sees intricacies of texture, I see cosmic warfare. Our different natures and giftings normally make us both better, a terrific team. But it was bad chemistry when "business" easily became 24/7. We shared so many joys and gifts over five years in Asia, but coleading was hard on our marriage.

During our time in Northeast Asia, I was responsible for guiding MCC's work in North Korea and led many teams there. Each visit required enormous time and preparation, and there are numerous risks visiting the country. Before one trip, North Korea began missile launches and ominous threats filled the headlines. But as life slowed down in Vermont, I realized that I had feared facing my family more than facing Pyongyang. Why was I more motivated to go to North Korea and face challenges there than go to North Carolina and face the brokenness in my private life?

Removed from my busy New York City schedule, separated from face-to-face friendships, sentenced to online worship, the landscape of my life was stripped of the familiar habits and forms of life that made me feel significant, competent, useful, grounded.

My public work was successful. It made me feel relevant, it gained praise, it was important. It gave me public validation. But so many private loses, letdowns, and tensions made me feel incompetent, sad, deenergized.

BEING FAITHFUL TO WHAT IS NEAR

As the unwelcome feelings kept crawling out, I found myself facing a truth I had learned years before in the Mississippi crisis with my colleague Spencer Perkins.

At the time, our public influence and acclaim was growing rapidly. But privately, so was our mutual bitterness. After a long personal conflict, our relationship stood on a precipice. Neither of us knew how to keep from going off the cliff.

God be praised—grace interrupted us and began to heal our relationship. That breakthrough didn't change our views on the importance of God's call to engage the toughest social challenges. We still believed that God's reconciliation is as big as healing race and poverty in America.

But we also learned a new truth: Yes, God "reconciles all things" (Colossians 1:20), and God's reconciliation is as big as healing race and poverty in America. Yet at the very same time, God's reconciliation is never bigger than the person nearest to you who is most difficult to love.

Sitting there in Vermont, God's peace was still as big as healing the divide between North Korea and South Korea, as big as the pandemic challenges facing the world. But God's peace was not bigger than healing within my family and marriage.

God's call is as big as healing the great challenges of our new global time. As big as facing rising global disparity, polarization, political mediocrity, and the themes of this book. Yet at the very same time, God's calling is never bigger than what is near to us. Never bigger than the unhealed relationships in our families, marriages, offices, pews. Never bigger than our own divided hearts. Never bigger than seeing and facing the truth of our private lives—our feelings, losses, and sins.

DISRUPTION AND INTERRUPTION

Times of disruption often expose unwelcome realities that are near to us and that we would rather not face—realities of our hearts, losses, griefs, and broken relationships.

During the pandemic, hidden behind big social media platforms, some of my friends began to see their marriages fall apart. Another friend gained great satisfaction from a job traveling to many countries, being constantly in the public eye. But when the pandemic hit, she was suddenly cut off from travel, trapped in daily life in a small apartment with her family. The longer they were together, the more unhealed memories and pains they had hidden from one another began to emerge.

As a group, few lives were disrupted more than pastors. So many hit the breaking point that 38 percent of them seriously considered quitting their pastoral profession.[1] For Seattle pastor Peter Chin, the usual heavy calling of leading a congregation became a "crushing calling." His new pastoral landscape was a "paralyzing degree of complexity and controversy [in] every single situation I face, every decision I make," a tense church climate in which "everyone is on a hair trigger, ready to walk away at the merest hint that the church does not line up with their political or personal perspectives." The new season of being a pastor, says Chin, is "fragmented, chaotic, and unclear." With the physical presence of personal relationships that normally provided strength and wisdom stripped away as well, Chin felt full of fear and bitterness.[2]

A severe disruption can throw us into a wilderness where we feel incompetent and without a roadmap to guide us. Stripped of the familiar, we see how much our hearts and lives are shaped by a search for public validation.

Thrust into the wilderness after his baptism, Jesus is weak and on unfamiliar ground. There the devil beckons Jesus with temptations—to turn stones into bread, to take control of all the kingdoms of the world, to jump off a cliff and be saved by angels. Pastor Peter Scazzero calls them "the great temptation to a false self"—temptations to believe "I am what I do. I am what I have. I am what others think of me."[3]

I am what I do. I am what I have. I am what others think of me. These are identities centered in public validation. I am what validates me in the public eye.

But in the wilderness, Jesus declared these identities to be false, and held onto his true identity as God's beloved son. The difficult ground of wilderness became holy ground that prepared him to launch a public ministry grounded in his true identity.

Disruptions can become places of divine interruption in our lives, stripping us of what is familiar, revealing false identities, and calling us to face what is in our hearts.

In a radical shift that would lead into the last eleven years of his life, Henri Nouwen found himself disrupted and disturbed after moving from teaching at Harvard University to living at a L'Arche community near Toronto, Canada, with people who have mental disabilities. Nouwen's identity was grounded in public achievements and acclaim over many prestigious years at Notre Dame, Yale, and Harvard. But thrust into the unfamiliar daily life among the residents of L'Arche, Nouwen discovered that "their liking or disliking me had absolutely nothing to do with any of the many useful things I had done until then." His academic skills, bestselling books, and fame brought him no relevance, popularity, or power at L'Arche. What he did, what he had, what others thought of him at Harvard had no validation at L'Arche.[4]

Stripped of a form of life that brought public validation, Nouwen found himself in a wilderness he didn't know how to navigate. "I was suddenly faced with my naked self," said Nouwen. "In a way, it seemed as though I was starting my life all over again."[5]

But the disruption of L'Arche became a time of divine inter-ruption in Nouwen's life. The people of L'Arche taught Nouwen excellence of the heart and excellence of life with those who were close to him. They taught him how to be centered in private integrity rather than public validation.

PUBLIC VALIDATION AND PRIVATE INTEGRITY

Public validation is "I am what I do. I am what I have. I am what others think of me." Some of us may only face one of those temptations. Whatever the case, habits that are formed by public validation are hazardous to private integrity.

By *private*, I mean who we are out of public view. Who we are with those who are nearest to us every day, who see and know what others do not see and know. They see what is in the hid-denness of our hearts, and who we are when nobody is looking. By *integrity*, I mean doing the right thing even when no one is watching. But even deeper than our actions, integrity is a state of being whole and undivided. It is honestly facing and healing what is in our hearts. Private integrity is living truthfully from the inside out.

Psalm 51:6 is a call to private integrity, saying of God: "Behold, you desire truth in the innermost being" (NASB). Private integrity is opening ourselves up to God honestly and fully. It is knowing our unseen, unwelcome, and broken parts, and bringing them before the mercy of God. In a sentence, what I mean by *private integrity* is this: honestly facing and healing what is near to us and hidden from public view—our hearts, feelings, losses, broken relationships, sins.

Public validation is centered in "I am what I do, what I have, and what others think of me." Private integrity is centered in "I am beloved without doing anything; I am what God thinks of me, and my public presence is fully integrated with integrity in what is near."

What obstacles block us from honestly facing what is near to us in our hearts, losses, broken relationships, and sins? I want to explore four—the lure of success, the shame of transparency, the scarcity of skills and structures, and the seduction of power.

THE LURE OF SUCCESS

One obstacle to private integrity is pouring the best of our time, energy, and growth into public validation.

In *The Second Mountain*, David Brooks tells of the professional acclaim and success he achieved as a *New York Times* columnist and TV commentator. But beneath that public success, he confesses, hidden from view, he "sidestepped the responsibilities of relationship." His patterns, Brooks says, were "sins of withdrawal: evasion, workaholism, conflict avoidance, failure to empathize, and a failure to express myself openly." When those he was close to were in need, he was too busy or too distant. He prioritized "time over people [and] productivity over relationship." In public life, Brooks was a master communicator. But his singular focus on achievement, writes Brooks, "turned me into a certain sort of person: aloof, invulnerable, and uncommunicative, at least when it came to my private life."[6]

Because of the power of "I am what I do, what I have, and what others think of me," we can easily become people of public excellence and private incompetence. As Brooks came to see, public success without private integrity is not only a divided life, it is a failed life. Success in life is as big as excellence in our professional life. Yet success is never bigger than our private integrity. An uninterrupted life of public success and private failure is a divided and infected life—it becomes cancerous in our hearts, relationships, and character.

THE SHAME OF TRANSPARENCY

A second obstacle to private integrity is the power of shame and guilt to prevent us from facing unwelcome truths about ourselves.

In my broken relationship with Spencer, it took a long time before I was willing to examine and give a name to one of the secrets of my heart. I didn't like how this secret made me feel, so I tried to deny it and push it away. But like one pesky mosquito becoming a swarm, it wouldn't stop coming. It was not easy for me to admit this unwelcome feeling was part of me. It was harder still to give it a name: *envy*. It was another challenge for me to tell Donna about the envy in my heart. But that envy increasingly poisoned my feelings toward Spencer and weighed me down with guilt and shame. And then I hit the breaking point. An incident happened in front of our entire Antioch community, and the secret envy of my heart was there for all to see. It was humiliating. I felt so out of control. So unable to solve my sin.

I'll never forget what happened next. As I sat there in a sobbing mess, fellow Antioch member Gloria Lotts rose from her seat, crossed the room, and embraced me. Gloria had experienced deep brokenness and liberation in her own life. Her embrace carried the powerful grace of a wounded healer.

My mentor John Alexander used to say, "Our sin is not interesting. We all sin. What is interesting is grace." Rather than hiding our shame out of a fear of humiliation, naming and confessing the truth of what is in our hearts in a community of trust can begin the journey of being liberated.

THE SCARCITY OF SKILLS AND STRUCTURES

The families, cultures, and institutions we are immersed in throughout our lives have a powerful influence on our growth in private integrity and whether we mature in honestly facing our feelings, losses, and brokenness.

Donna and I are both descendants of cultural traditions that don't "do grief." Funerals were calm assemblies that conveyed a message of "they're in a better place—so good lord, please act like it."

Our dominant institutions of education and work are rarely designed to form us in vulnerability. Every institution has what I call its *charism*, their unique and special gifts and vocation available for the good of the reign of God. But every institution also has its *captivity*, the unique ways in which it is captive to powers that hinder or resist the reign of God.

One time Duke Divinity School offered me a job, and at the same time MCC offered a position to me and Donna in Africa. When I met with a faculty member to help me discern, he said, "Well, if you go with MCC you'll become a holier person." While the academic world has many gifts, especially at the Duke level it's an elite, hierarchical, hypercompetitive world of systems and incentives that reward individual performance and can put the so-called best and brightest on a pedestal of adulation. There are no systems in place to check hubris at the door and cultivate habits of vulnerability and community. The longer you're immersed, the easier it is to become captive.

Not only our families and workplaces, but many of our churches, too, rarely form us in skills and habits of honest interior examination. During the first pandemic year I took a church class called "Emotionally Healthy Spirituality." The title itself was jarring to me. There is endless focus in our society on physical, intellectual, social, and spiritual health. But in my decades of Christian life and six years of seminary education, I can't remember a pastor, professor, or church talk about emotional health. That class opened a new frontier in my spiritual growth and came at a critical moment in my wilderness journey facing the pain in my family.

THE SEDUCTION OF POWER

In recent years, numerous celebrated Christian institutions have been tarnished by abuses of power and sexual misconduct at the leadership level—from Willow Creek Community Church, to Ravi Zacharias International Ministries, to Mars Hill Church. Adding enormous pain and shame is nearly six thousand Catholic priests accused of sexual abuse in the United States alone, along with institutional complicity and cover up.

Most painful for me is the story of Jean Vanier. While I was serving at the Duke Center for Reconciliation, Vanier was one of my inspirations. He had founded L'Arche, the international federation of communities of people with mental disabilities that Henri Nouwen joined after leaving Harvard. Vanier's writings on spirituality, leadership as servanthood, and mission as mutuality had a profound influence on our work. Duke developed a summer field education partnership with L'Arche, sending students to live and serve at the same community near Toronto, Canada, where Nouwen had lived.

When we invited Vanier to Duke for a weekend of teaching, he enthusiastically accepted. In a typically L'Arche way, an entire L'Arche community from Virginia joined him for a weekend of public events, lectures, and meals. The highlight was the worship service, when L'Arche led us in a footwashing liturgy, a sacred practice in their communities. What a sight it was: Duke University, the height of academia, interrupted by the mix of wheelchairs, basins of water, towels, and tears.

When Jean Vanier passed away in 2019 at age ninety, I mourned. A year later when shocking revelations emerged, I was devastated.

An internal report by L'Arche found that Vanier had sexually abused six women over thirty-five years. They reported that Vanier had been manipulative and emotionally abusive and initiated sexual relations during private times of giving spiritual guidance. Vanier asked the women to keep what happened secret.[7]

I cannot reconcile the gentle, public Vanier I met at Duke and the private Vanier. The man who formed an institution rooted in servanthood and vulnerability, and the man who abused his power to manipulate and satisfy himself at great harm to others. No one knows the secrets of his heart.

What I do know is that power without interior integrity is exceedingly dangerous. What I also know is that protecting against abuse is not a private matter but an institutional responsibility. In the cases of abuse I named, we see a volatile recipe of men in positions of enormous emotional, spiritual, and organizational power, put on a pedestal by their followers, with insufficient structures of accountability. Power without communal safeguarding is exceedingly dangerous.

A THEOLOGY OF VULNERABILITY AND SAFEGUARDING

In the Bible the wilderness is a place of vulnerability—of wrestling with God (Jacob), deprivation (Elijah), danger (Hagar and Ismael), and temptation (Jesus after his baptism). Yet in the fragility of the wilderness Isaiah heard this promise from God: "I'm there to be found" (Isaiah 41:17-20, as translated by Eugene Peterson in *The Message*). *Right there,* in the barren hills, says God, "I'll open up rivers" and "I'll place the cypress in the desert" (vv. 18-19). God's promise to Isaiah is, I'm at work in the wilderness. God is not found on the other side of vulnerability, but in it.

Places of vulnerability can become places of divine interruption—Elijah hearing the still small voice, Moses' encounter with the burning bush, Jesus being ministered to by angels. The pathway to find God lies through our vulnerability.

Not long after Spencer died, another member of our Antioch community discovered she had a serious cancer. It was just too much for us all. Losing Spencer, and now possibly losing another of our precious companions? As we gathered around our beloved friend and began to pray, my feelings of helplessness and anger rose up out of nowhere. I spontaneously shouted out, "God, *we* can't do anything about this. God, *you* have a problem! This is *your* problem. We beg you, heal our dear sister!"

God, you have a problem. At the time, I felt unspiritual and uncomfortable saying that. But I no longer shy away from sharing my honest feelings with God.

We can draw strength from the vulnerability of Jesus. In the Gospels, his honest emotions are laid bare for all to see. Clearing tables at the temple, his anger. Sitting with Mary, his delight. Learning of the death of his friend Lazarus, his grief. On the cross, his cry of agony and abandonment. As his disciples battle over who is the greatest, his frustration. Above all, throughout his ministry—even in his last meal with his disciples before his death—his joy: "I have told you this so that my joy may be in you and that your joy may be complete" (John 15:11 NIV).

With God and with his followers, Jesus shares his feelings honestly, openly, freely. Surely the psalms of the Bible lived deeply within him. The twin sisters of the psalms are wild praise and the agony of lament, always walking hand in hand. In *Getting Involved with God*, biblical scholar Ellen Davis explains that in the Bible, only the psalms "are clearly formulated as human speech, packaged ready to be put directly into our mouths." Indeed, "the most important thing about the Psalms [is] they are undisguisedly human utterances."[8]

The psalmists are our masters in teaching us how, in the desolate places of our lives, vulnerability turns barren ground into fertile soil for meeting God. There is no psalm greater than David's cry of Psalm 51 to teach us the way to vulnerability—to see, express, and confess the truth that is in our hearts. Three times David speaks of the heart, that seat of our deepest feelings and vulnerability:

> You desire truth in the inward being;
>> therefore teach me wisdom in my secret heart.
> Create in me a clean heart, O God,
>> and put a new and right spirit within me.
> The sacrifice acceptable to God is a broken spirit;
>> a broken and contrite heart, O God, you will not despise.
> (Psalm 51:6, 10, 17 NRSVue)

A wise heart, a clean heart, a broken heart—God desires truthfulness from the inside out. As Davis writes, "We cannot have an intimate relationship with someone to whom we cannot speak honestly. That is what the Psalms are about: speaking our mind honestly and fully before God."[9] There is no intimacy with God without vulnerability with God.

The psalms teach us the disturbing yet revolutionary power of owning and naming our honest feelings to God in ways that, as Davis writes, "would seem to violate all the rules for Christian prayer."[10]

One year in Uganda, at the institute that the Duke Center for Reconciliation helped start in East Africa, Dr. Bungishabaku Katho taught from Jeremiah on the biblical practice of lament. He spoke of Jeremiah's honest feelings and then, following that example, named specific problems in the region and his own honest lamentations of frustration and anger with God and with the church. The whole time, the room of 150 participants was tense.

A colleague took me aside during tea break. "Here, when Christians deal with God, we think God expects me to be loving, calm. So people cannot say what is in their heart. They rebel. This morning was countercultural, asking them to do the unthinkable. You almost cease to be yourself."

Being specific about our feelings breaks revolutionary new terrain of vulnerability. As Davis explains, "The Psalms give us words for all the moods in which we come before God: adulation, exultation, gratitude; but also rage, despair, fear—those feelings which, as 'saints,' we feel required to deny."[11]

Psalm 51 teaches us that a vulnerable heart is a courageous heart that breaks over sin. But here is what happens: "When we let our hearts break before God," writes Davis, "the pieces do not sink into oblivion. They are borne up, they float, yes, they sail on the tide of God's mercy."[12]

Integrity has a vulnerable and honest heart. An honest heart is a breaking heart. And only a broken and contrite heart can become a healed heart, sailing on the mercy of God.

PRACTICAL STEPS TOWARD PRIVATE INTEGRITY

Public validation is centered in "I am what I do, what I have, and what others think of me." Private integrity is honestly facing and healing what is near to us and hidden from public view—our hearts, losses, broken relationships, sins. Four practical steps you can take are fearless interior examination, being vulnerable with trusted companions, communal safeguarding, and faithfully attending to the details of what's near.

Fearless interior examination. Not far from the UN building and close to my office is Dag Hammarskjöld Plaza, a beautiful oasis in Manhattan where I often eat lunch. Hammarskjöld was a Swedish economist and diplomat who served as the second secretary-general leading the United Nations. He was also a person of deep Christian faith. His private journal was published after he died in a plane crash. Titled *Markings*, it is deeply spiritual writing. Reading it, you'd never know Hammarskjöld is world famous, shuttling between the world's worst conflicts. The journal is a fearless examination of his inner life. He names what he sees in his heart—greed for power, pretentiousness and envy, self-conceit, love of flattery. Once he wrote this warning to himself: "Never let success hide its emptiness from you, achievement its nothingness, toil its desolation. And so keep alive the incentive to push on further, that pain in the soul which drives us beyond ourselves."[13]

In the church class I took on emotionally healthy spirituality, Pastor Rich Villodas said, "Our reactions are an important source of revelation for our lives."[14] The journey of private integrity depends on specifically identifying, processing, expressing, and confessing our honest feelings, losses, and joys. In fact, often our reaction to what others do says more about us than about them.

We learned two steps I recommend for interior examination of feelings and reactions. First, use these four questions on a regular basis as a guide to interior examination: What are you mad about? What are you sad about? What are you anxious about? What are you glad about? Own the feelings, discuss them with a trusted friend, voice them to God, and reflect with a mentor on what happens as a result of this process. Second, when an incident happens that disturbs you, ask yourself these questions: What happened? What am I feeling? What is the story I'm telling myself? What does the gospel say? What counterinstinctual action is needed?[15]

Be vulnerable with trusted companions. When Seattle pastor Peter Chin hit the breaking point during the pandemic, a single word in Psalm 13 rescued him: "But I trust in your unfailing love (*chesed*)" (Psalm 13:5 NIV). *Chesed*, writes Chin, "is how God loves his people—with an enduring and faithful love that transcends circumstances and seasons." In the book of Ruth, *chesed* is used between people—seen in the care and generosity between Naomi and her daughters-in-law, and Ruth and Boaz. "So this loyal, unfailing love," writes Chin, "is not only something that we receive from God; *chesed* is also how we are called to love others."[16]

One way to grow in private integrity is to expose your heart honestly to trusted companions. I've received so much *chesed* from mentors through words they spoke to me in crises, words that live deep in my soul, and that I still beckon forth to correct and redirect my heart and mind in the now.

When my envy became public, Gloria's hug in front of our entire Antioch community was a revelation of grace that told me, "Don't worry. We all sin. I'm here to walk with you."

Gordon Loux served as a consultant to us during some organizational challenges in Mississippi. I remember his organizational advice, but his personal wisdom is ingrained in my soul. I told Gordon I felt like I was playing second fiddle to Spencer, and how it made me feel. Gordon had served as the first president of Prison Fellowship, working alongside visionary founder Chuck Colson. As a well-known public figure who had worked in the Nixon White House and wrote a best-selling book, Colson got the public credit. Gordon struggled with that. But he came to peace with it, and I have called on his words many times: "What's most important is influence, not visibility. Keep your eye on the mission, not recognition." As someone with many privileges in life, that is a word I need to hear.

In the devastating aftermath of Spencer's sudden death, my grief counselor, Cille Norman, asked that question that steered my life in a whole new direction, a question I still ask at critical turning points: "What idea of the future fills your heart with joy?"

After leaving Mississippi, Donna and I wrestled with where we should live and where I should go to seminary. As we shared our anxious hearts with John and Judy Alexander, out of nowhere, John said, "Go to Duke. I have friends there who will take care of you." We believed John. We moved to Durham. And his friends did take care of us.

During an organizational crisis at Duke, trying to defend my public validation like a relentless lawyer, I visited St. Francis Springs and shared my feelings of anger and failure with Father Louie. And after hearing my sob story, his response: "What an opportunity!" Without those words, I don't know if I would have been able to give up Duke and, with Donna, cross the world to serve in Korea.

How would I have found my way forward without trusted companions like Gloria, Gordon, Cille, John and Judy, and Father Louie? When we make our hearts vulnerable in the wilderness, it is trusted companions who help us find Jesus and our true self.

Communal safeguarding. Jean Vanier's sin damaged the women he abused and devastated the community he founded. But instead of fleeing from organizational brokenness, L'Arche leadership conducted a thorough investigation, publicly published its findings, and adopted new safeguarding standards. They invited L'Arche staff and members to see, name, and feel the brokenness and the "shadow side" of L'Arche *as a community*.

Every congregation and Christian institution should lead the way in what L'Arche calls safeguarding, not only "protecting people from harm" but also "preventing and responding to harm caused by neglect, personal abuse, exploitation, violence, and/or harassment (including when these are sexual in nature)."[17]

Every organization is always prodigal in some respects, giving in to temptations, hubris, and blind positivity. Christian ethicist Nancy Duff argues that the minimal attention in the church to embracing negativity, as well as the "self-deceptive refusal to acknowledge things for how they really are," calls for the recovery of lament as a practice in Christian liturgy.[18]

We would do well to practice lament institutionally as a means of renewal and safeguarding. One organization I have seen practice institutional lament is InterVarsity Christian Fellowship. InterVarsity is one of the 400 largest US nonprofits, with an annual budget of $100 million, more than 1,500 staff, and presence on 600 campuses. InterVarsity is unusual in being a highly professional organization with a proven capacity for self-correction.

But around 2005, when a set of individual and system failures occurred that caused pain and tension between Asian American and African American staff, it sent ripples throughout the organization. For years, the wounds lingered yet were not ignored.

Paula Fuller, InterVarsity's vice president for multiethnic ministry explained: "If we're going to create witnessing communities on campus that are growing in love for every ethnicity, we can't do that if we're not living out that commitment as an organization." Fuller said InterVarsity has a tradition of engaging its organizational sins. "Following Christ is difficult. You're crucifying your flesh," Fuller said. "This mantle has been passed by those who came before."

Five years later, InterVarsity's president and cabinet traveled for five days to the 2010 Duke Summer Reconciliation Institute in hope of addressing the unresolved wounds and to search for a theological paradigm for taking multiethnic ministry into deeper maturity. They discovered this in the biblical discipline of lament, a way of owning brokenness without expecting that it can be immediately solved or fixed.[19]

At Duke, together as a multiracial team, InterVarsity's top leaders acknowledged that the organization was crippled. Fuller believes the lack of a theology of failure has conditioned leaders, staff, and donors "to only think of success, of things going right. When things are bad, the most we do is sing a praise song through clenched teeth." The gift of lament, she said, opened a new avenue of healing for InterVarsity.[20] In the following years InterVarsity leaned into the practice of lament as it wrestled with issues of racial injustice, sexuality, and organizational change.

Private integrity is deeply influenced by institutional integrity and depends not only on personal vulnerability but also on institutional vulnerability. When did your workplace last lead a seminar on that topic?

Caring, forgiving, and keeping the dishes washed. When the drive for public success becomes primary in our lives, squeezes out what is near, and gets the best of our time and habits, living differently begins with a different mantra than bestselling books like *The Magic of Thinking Big, How to Win Friends and Influence People,* and *Good to Great.*

When he was leading the United Nations, Dag Hammar-skjöld wrote the following in his journal: "The 'great' commitment all too easily obscures the 'little' one."[21] Bigger is not better. At many times, the faithful movement of Christian maturity in our lives is not from good to great, but from great to little.

After Spencer died of a heart attack at age forty-four, the Antioch community was in turmoil. In many ways Spencer was the shepherd of our life together—as pastor, as visionary, as peacemaker, as the one most dedicated to herding our stubborn selves into maturity. Thrust into a wilderness, we didn't know the way forward.

Our mentors John and Judy Alexander came from San Francisco to support Antioch in our crisis. They advised us to slow down, take time to grieve, and not make any big decisions for a while. They said something was far more important than deciding whether Antioch should continue or disband.

"Here's what we think you should focus on at this time," said John. "Caring for each other, forgiving each other, and keeping the dishes washed. The rest is details."

When our hearts are filled with anxiety regarding life, work, the future, it is easy to lose sight of what is primary. Sometimes the best step to address matters of public importance that everyone sees is to address the matters of private importance that no one sees. John and Judy offer us a vision of what is enough. It is enough to care for each other, to forgive each other, and to keep the dishes washed.

"LET IT BE TO ME ACCORDING TO YOUR WORD"

Early in the pandemic in Vermont, my usual United Nations and New York City routines brought to a standstill, I had claimed those words of Mary. So what was God's word to me?

Gradually, sharing daily rhythms with Dad on our little monastic compound, I realized the word was right in front of me.

At evening meals, I listened to Dad's stories (many more than once). Watched his eyes light up, still thrilled by photos of his beloved Sue, my mother, who had passed away two years earlier. Heard him break easily into Korean language, still flowing from his sixteen years of service there. Saw into the mind of a preacher, coming alive whenever stories from the Bible became the topic. Felt the heart of a pastor, opening up in many drives together across the nearby hills. He knew every house and held in confidence its secrets of pain and hope, homes where he had entered, listened, prayed, and healed. I urgently arranged a video conference call with my siblings so he could share his anxiety about moving into a retirement community—and he showed up with an opening prayer, a minisermon, and a closing exhortation (to himself), as if in front of a congregation once again.

I cared for Dad. In my long separation from Donna, he cared for me. It was not always easy. I had to forgive him, and he me, many times. And the dishes? I cooked, he did the dishes. And then I did them a bit more.

Over those four months, my work disrupted, healing somehow came with my children and with my siblings. Traveling that terrain in life with Dad, I realized "this is the word." Right there on that small plot, unexpected ground became holy ground.

Dad was brave. He did move into the retirement community. But he didn't make it to the end of the year. In December he passed away. What a gift to be with my brother at his bedside. And what a precious gift to be near my father in his final year of life.

Is anything in life bigger than that?

CHAPTER SEVEN

Cultivating Moral Imagination for a World of Unprecedented Dangers

There is a realm of time where the goal is not to have but to be, not to own but to give, not to control but to share, not to subdue but to be in accord. Life goes wrong when the control of space, the acquisition of things of space, becomes our sole concern.

ABRAHAM HESCHEL, *THE SABBATH*

Three great dangers accelerated in power during the pandemic—a bipolar China–United States world, environmental decay, and technological disruption. I speak of them together because of what they have in common. Whether or not we are aware, they now affect every life and corner of our world in three ways.

First, their power is inescapable. Wherever we live, every one of us is affected. Second, these dangers are existential. They threaten our collective survival and well-being as human beings who share a common home on this planet. Third, unlike most of the other challenges in this book, these three dangers are unprecedented. They are new to human history in the sense that their harmful impact is keenly felt only now in the twenty-first century and with increasing danger in the decades ahead.

When it comes to these dangers, many in my generation come from a time of innocence. For us, climate change was a drive from Vermont to Florida. Big tech was getting the first, and very adorable, Apple Macintosh computer, with a fat 128K of memory (I remember telling a colleague "500K? No, we don't need extra memory; we'll never use it"). When I studied the Mandarin Chinese language in college, Americans couldn't travel to China. Later, when China opened up its country and economy in the 1980s, there was great optimism about a new era of freedom unfolding there, with hope of Americans and Chinese leading the way in a post–Cold War world. The fall of the Berlin Wall in 1989 signaled that the Soviet Union might be next.

The age of innocence is over; a new age has begun. Regarding climate, technology, and China, here are some glimpses of the new time of danger each presents to our lives—seen in technological disruption, environmental decay, and a battle for dominance between the two superpowers of China and the United States. While such challenges call for big responses, I will follow up the three dangers with practical application grounded in a different "think little" approach, which is equally important.

THE FIRST DANGER: TECHNOLOGICAL DISRUPTION

Technological innovation has brought immense and obvious benefits; digital highways are now as important as physical highways, and there will be more changes in the next twenty years than in the last hundred. Few people in the world, including some of the most vulnerable, don't find their cellphone indispensable. But with progress often comes a techno-optimism that denies the harmful power of technological disruption over our lives. As computer technology expert Peter Robinson writes,

"Few technologies are devised with malicious intent, but most technologies can be turned to malicious use."[1] While harmful consequences are not always intended, they are real in the form of data power, dopamine, dystopian reality, and division.

Data power. Life is digital. With our phones becoming computers, we feel more powerful. But every time we scroll or click, power is exercised over us. Big tech giants Amazon, Apple, Facebook, Google, and Microsoft seize our private data and transform us from users into profitable products. Data is the new oil, and it is controlled by only a few countries and companies, mostly in the United States and China.

Dopamine. Testifying before Congress, Facebook whistleblower Frances Haugen said the company was fully aware of damaging the mental health of children and teenagers. Haugen spoke of "little feedback loops" in which "likes and comments and re-shares" trigger "hits of dopamine to your friends so they will create more content."[2] Dopamine is a chemical produced in the brain that is associated with feelings of pleasure and reward. Dr. Anna Lembke, psychiatrist and professor at Stanford University and author of *Dopamine Nation: Finding Balance in the Age of Indulgence*, considers dopamine to be an addictive substance. The smartphone, she says, "is the equivalent of the hypodermic needle for a wired generation."[3] A new class of electronic pleasures are engineered to be addictive and, in excess, lead to depression, anxiety, and enormous profits for social media companies—texting, tweeting, surfing the web, online shopping, gambling, and posting. And let's face it, most Christians spend more time on social media than receiving biblical teaching.

Dystopian reality. Consult Siri or Alexa, make a U-turn as told by the GPS, open your phone with face ID, read personalized feeds on your phone—behind it all is the power of artificial intelligence (AI). In China, where face-recognition is used to control Muslim Uyghur people, Vinoth Ramachandra describes what sounds like a page from the "Big Brother" world of George Orwell's 1984:

> But the wider aim is to collect as much information as possible about every company and citizen in the entire country, store it in a centralized database and assign a credit score to both companies and citizens that indicates how "trustworthy" they are. This is a draconian form of social discipline, designed to identify and punish human rights activists, political dissidents and other so-called "anti-social elements" by denying them and their family members employment, housing, banking services and other social benefits.[4]

China's ambition is to dominate global artificial intelligence by greatly expanding research and education.

Division. Misinformation, disinformation, and algorithms that rule what we read and don't read make it difficult to separate truth from propaganda. The information flood of our time doesn't make us wiser, but it certainly makes us more divided. *Christianity Today* columnist Bonnie Kristian says she is "increasingly convinced the sheer availability of content (particularly political content designed to inflame our worst passions) may be the most unprecedented challenge in Christian discipleship today."[5]

THE SECOND DANGER: ENVIRONMENTAL DECAY

The earth, our common home with people, animals, and plants, is experiencing long-term shifts in weather patterns. Severe weather, droughts, and floods are more frequent and happen in new places. Wildfires are filling skies in the western United States and Canada so much that there is a dreaded new time of year called "smoke season."

Environmental decay harms people. It negatively affects our everyday life, including access to healthy food and clean air and water. For many in the world, environmental decay affects their ability to work and live in their home communities. New pandemics are a threat. While their origin is in microbes carried by animals, their emergence is driven by human activities. Wildlife, livestock, and people are coming into closer contact with each other, allowing animal microbes to move into people. These activities include agricultural expansion and wildlife trade. This leads to infections, sometimes outbreaks, and more rarely into true pandemics that spread through road networks, global travel, and densely populated places.

Environmental decay harms God's creation. Economies and lifestyles are still dominated by a "take, make, waste" approach, which causes more and more harm to our common home. According to the World Wildlife Fund, human activities have caused us to lose two-thirds of the world's wildlife population in the last fifty years.[6]

Environmental decay affects people unequally. Those who suffer most are also those least responsible for the crisis to date: people in countries and places that are already vulnerable because of lack of power, discrimination, or poverty. In one rural Kenya community, facing the worst drought in decades, their livestock is dying, children lack sufficient milk, and farmers carry automatic weapons to guard against invading pastoralists from Uganda fighting for scarce water.[7] For communities like this, climate change is bringing immediate and visceral harm—less food and water, loss of valuable livestock, reduced income, and migrating to find employment.

Environmental decay is rooted in human lifestyles. As Ramachandra writes:

> It is our unsustainable global consumption habits, driven by demand in developed countries and emerging economies, as well as by demographic pressure, that must change. Scientific and economic analysis warns that unless we make transformative changes in our taken-for-granted "lifestyles," the costs of climate change coupled with more regular pandemics will . . . [be] more dangerous than what we are currently experiencing.[8]

THE THIRD DANGER: A BIPOLAR CHINA-VERSUS-US WORLD

The United States is no longer the only superpower in the world, and the relationship between China and the United States will affect the entire planet for decades to come, for better or worse. Four key dynamics include China's growing confidence, power, and police state, and the United States–China rivalry.

Growing confidence. Myrrl Byler, the executive director of Mennonite Partners in China (MPC), has engaged China for over thirty years. Myrrl tells how a Chinese friend, a professor, once picked him up at the Beijing airport in a brand-new BMW. "I never ever dreamed I would be able to own a car!" he told Myrrl. "For the first forty years of my life, it was something I just never thought about." China's amazing material progress has lifted nearly 800 million people out of poverty in just one generation, bringing a new identity for many who moved into the new middle or upper classes. "From a century of humiliation, they are now in a century of confidence," says Myrrl. "They feel good about their country and their future. They feel ready to have equal footing in the world."[9]

Growing superpower. In airports in Africa, I saw many short-term mission groups from churches in the United States—often all wearing the same T-shirt proclaiming their cause. But in the late 2000s I began to notice as many groups of Chinese people. They were on a kind of mission too—to build highways, buildings, infrastructure, and extend China's global reach. My friends doing development and church work in Africa, Asia, and Latin America testify that Chinese presence and power is becoming pervasive. While the infrastructure China brings is needed, it comes with significant negative consequences, from hard-to-pay loans to being politically beholden to China.

Growing police state. Although it was largely overlooked, China's seizure of complete control of Hong Kong in 2020 was hugely significant, ending free elections and free speech and breaking the hearts of my treasured friends there. Within China itself, while the majority is very happy with what the government has done for them through remarkable material progress and growing global influence, it is more and more becoming a police state, and the control and surveillance over the population and the church is enormous. Xi Lian of Duke Divinity School says the Communist Party sees Christianity as a unique threat because its "transcendent vision and transcendent values" present the Party with a formidable "moral and ideological rivalry."[10]

US–China animosity. My work with the United Nations gives me a front-row seat to battles between the United States and China on the Security Council, and the resulting paralysis in addressing global challenges. In a 2021 Gallup poll, Americans named China as their country's greatest enemy, doubling the percentage from a year earlier.[11] Attitudes on both sides point to rising tension and competition. It is terrifying that whenever this happens, Asian Americans are blamed and attacked in the United States, with over ten thousand hate incidents reported from March 2020 to December 2021, the majority taking place in public spaces.[12] As Christian sociologist Russell Jeung, founder of Stop AAPI Hate, explains:

> Sometimes [we Asian Americans] are the model minority. Two years ago, we were Crazy Rich Asians and beloved. But in times of war, in times of pandemic, in times of economic downturn, we're pushed out from being insider to America to being outsiders of America. And so we're seen as perpetual foreigners.[13]

Unless change happens, the more China is hated, the more Asian Americans are hated and ostracized as well.

BEYOND TECHNICAL SOLUTIONS

The challenges of technological disruption, environmental decay, and a bipolar world are complex and hotly debated. Many good books and resources are available on the science, politics, and economics of these dangers.

But I want to look at these three challenges through a moral lens to examine their deeper roots. This requires going beyond technical solutions.

My wife Donna served many years as a home health nurse. When one of her homebound patients had a wound that was not healing, Donna knew how to heal the physical wound. She had the technical knowledge to *do things right*. But some of her patients were very difficult people, and others were in broken family situations. Healing also depended on *doing the right things*: healing hearts and relationships, anger and fear and neglect. She became skilled in the arts of attentiveness and relationship, attending to the patient's state of heart and mind, family situation, connection to community. She spent hours listening to their stories. She took time to get to know other family members living in the home.

Donna is committed to wholeness of life for her patients. She knows not only how to *do things right* but also to *do the right things*. And as a follower of Christ who prays daily for her patients and seeks to relate to them in the way of Christ, she has also learned to see and do the *faithful things*. Technically, she is a highly skilled nurse, and healing physical wounds matters greatly. But she is more than a nurse. She is a minister of good news. Many times, her patients were lifted into a new dimension of flourishing.

Great social challenges are more than technical problems. Science was critical to addressing Covid-19—hospitals, tests, vaccinations. But science cannot solve the problems of blame, fear, and division. Technical excellence is not enough to battle pandemics because fear and blame are not technical problems.

It's important to do things right, to be technically excellent. But if we don't do the right things, the tree prospers while the forest goes to rot, so to speak. And if we don't attend to the faithful things, we miss the deeper vision and pathway of change that God desires, including how we ourselves need to be changed.

Addressing technological disruption, environmental decay, and a bipolar world requires critical technical knowledge from many fields. But a deeper moral vision identifies a dangerous characteristic they share—seen in the story of Congo, cobalt, electric cars, and a battle for dominance between China and the United States.

THE LUST FOR DOMINION

You might not realize how close you are at this very moment to the shiny gray mineral known as cobalt. Every smartphone, laptop, and electric vehicle uses cobalt, essential for their lithium-ion batteries and key to boosting battery life. Indeed, the company Apple is the one of the world's biggest users of cobalt.

Cobalt doesn't grow on trees. More than two-thirds of the world's supply comes from the Democratic Republic of the Congo (DRC) in East Africa. With electric cars being critical to the world's clean energy economy and its vast profits, the Congo is a central battleground between China and the United States to dominate that economy. Big tech companies like Apple and big electric car makers like Tesla make huge profits from Congolese cobalt.

If only Congolese people benefited. Cobalt mining is haphazard and unregulated, more like a battle on a Wild West frontier. And as a proverb of the Kikuyu people of Kenya says, "When two elephants fight, it is the grass that is trampled." Vast cobalt mines tear apart the land and displace thousands of local people. The DRC is one of the world's most beautiful and richly resourced countries—a land of vast forests, mountains, lakes, and animals. But it is also one of the poorest and most conflict-ridden countries, exploited for centuries by greater powers seeking dominance, from Belgium in the twentieth century to Apple, Tesla, China, and the United States today.[14] The areas of cobalt mining, camps of displaced people, and locations of intense civilian killing overlap. The chilling contradiction is that as the green economy grows, so may the numbers of displaced people and deaths.

This story is only one of the many signs of the global contest for domination between the United States and China. This bipolar battle, technological disruption, and environmental decay—the harmful characteristic these dangers share, revealed in the story of cobalt, is a lust for dominance through might and material progress.

The church has a spotty record in countering the lust for dominance. A seminary professor of mine used to say, "We can quote the Bible and be unbiblical." One of the most harmful misinterpretations of Scripture is Genesis 1:26 and 1:28 where English translations say that God intended humans to "reign," "rule," or "have dominion" over living things. As Ellen Davis writes, "Since the Renaissance, Genesis 1:26 has frequently been invoked in the West to support the project of 'conquering,' 'commanding,' or 'enslaving' nature through scientific and technological means."[15] Not to mention "doctrines of discovery" whereby a heretical vision of God-given "dominion" was used to bless and justify the seizure of land from indigenous peoples, to colonize other countries and their natural resources, and to systematically kill and exploit entire groups of people.

The vision of dominion is one in which nature, land, and "weaker" people are viewed primarily as a source of profit and power. It is a vison where might makes right and material progress is the measure of human progress. Along the way, God's creation is maimed and the marginalized are most harmed.

It is noteworthy that China and the United States are not only the world's two biggest polluters and producers of carbon dioxide, but the two dominant powers in big data and artificial intelligence. Dominion is driven by the lust of very powerful forces. But as the great Jewish American theologian and social activist Abraham Heschel said, "some are guilty, but all are responsible." Every time you and I text, call, scroll, surf the web, or ride in a lithium-battery car, we benefit from Congolese cobalt.

MORAL IMAGINATION AND GOD'S SHALOM

How can we interrupt the lust for dominion?

One global pioneer in the field of peace studies is the Mennonite scholar John Paul Lederach. His first groundbreaking book, *Building Peace,* was about how to do things right to make peace happen. But twelve years later, Lederach said that approach—what he called the "engineering of social change"—was fundamentally flawed. The "evolution of [peacebuilding] becoming a profession, the orientation toward technique, and the management of process in conflict resolution," wrote Lederach, "have overshadowed . . . the heart and soul of constructive change."

Lederach's new book was not focused on technique and skill. Instead, he said deep change requires what he called the *moral imagination,* namely, "The capacity to imagine something rooted in the challenge of the real world yet capable of giving birth to that which does not yet exist."[16] Facing the challenge of the lust for dominance at the root of technological disruption, environmental decay, and a bipolar world, what different and better reality can a moral imagination help us see and give birth to?

Because those who are dominated often see more deeply, the marginalized world is often a source of moral imagination.

In contrast to the lust for dominion, for example, listen to this wildly different imagination in the wisdom of Black Elk of the Oglala Lakota Sioux people of the Great Plains.

> For Black Elk, his story could not be disconnected from a bigger story: "It is the story of all life that is holy and it is good to tell, and of us two-leggeds sharing in it with the four-leggeds and the wings of the air and all green things. . . ." Of a vision that came to him as a child, he said: "I saw that the sacred hoop of my people was one of many hoops that made one circle, wide as daylight and as starlight, and in the center grew one mighty flowering tree to shelter all the children of one mother and father. And I saw that it was holy."[17]

In Native American culture, explains theologian Randy Woodley, a hoop—as a circle connecting all things—is a common way of viewing life, representing the wholeness and interdependence of creation in the natural world.[18] Without being biblical, Black Elk voiced God's truth far more deeply than those who quoted the Bible while violently removing his people from their land. Dominion as domination, as Ellen Davis writes, "is unlike anything the biblical writers (or their premodern readers) could have imagined."[19] The biblical alternative to dominion is *shalom*, a vision not to conquer the earth but to care for it, as God does. Listen to Psalm 36:

> O Lord in the heavens is your steadfast love
> Your faithfulness to the clouds,
> Your righteousness is like the mighty mountains,
> Your acts of justice a great deep.
> Human and animals you save O LORD.[20]

Shalom is all the pieces of life, heaven and earth, woven into wholeness—God's love and righteousness, God's justice, God's care for all living beings, what Davis calls "God's covenantal commitment to creatures both human and non-human."

Dominion sacrifices principle for power and material progress, making them an end in themselves. But God's shalom overcomes a lust for control with a longing for communion. As Davis writes, "the Bible's own perspective is both material and spiritual; the wholeness (shalom) of the human heart and spirit is inseparable from the wellbeing (also shalom) of the physical world." Indeed, she continues, the "wellbeing of the earth depends on the integrity of the human heart" and "the Old Testament bespeaks throughout an intimacy with the land that is inseparable from Israel's intimacy with God."

Biblical shalom cannot be reduced to personal peace with God nor, on the other hand, to socioeconomic justice. Rather, shalom connects all of them together into a whole—heart, justice, care of creation, God's peace.

INSTILLING HOPE

Facing the lust for dominion, it's not easy to imagine change. Jane Goodall has spent a lifetime warning us about endangered creatures from the Tanzanian chimpanzee to the Florida manatee. She laments that in the last forty years we have lost about half of all the wild animal species on earth.

But warnings are not Goodall's priority. "Yes, we absolutely need to know all the doom and gloom," she says, "because we are approaching a crossroads, and if we don't take action it could be too late." But Goodall believes her calling is to give people hope. Traveling the world, she has seen animals saved from extinction by courageous efforts of people who do not give up.

When it comes to the great problems of our world, without hope we are immobilized. Stories of hope "should have equal time," Goodall says, because "If you don't have hope, why bother? Why should I bother to think about my ecological footprint if I don't think that what I do is going to make a difference? Why not eat, drink and be merry, for tomorrow we die?"[21]

Traveling in many places of brokenness, my hosts eventually tell a story about their "why bother" moment. At a difficult time they asked themselves, "Why should I bother if I cannot stop this division, end this discrimination, stop this war?"

That's why I am always sure to ask: "Where do you see hope? Where do you see people who are restless for a new reality?" After a moment, their faces always come alive. For here's what people working in the most difficult places have taught me: the way things are is not the way things have to be. God is always planting seeds of hope in the most broken places.

Regarding the unprecedented dangers of technological disruption, environmental decay, and the China-US bipolar battle for dominance, instilling hope is primary to our work in this new time. If one dangerous characteristic they share is a lust for dominance, and if God's shalom interrupts that lust, then what actions flow from that moral imagination?

Just as we need to deepen our understanding of the danger, we also need to deepen our imagination of hope.

THINK LITTLE

Lament and hope are closely related, and I am not one to minimize the scale of a problem. Indeed, technological disruption, environmental decay, and the superpower battle for dominance are what experts call "wicked problems."

A wicked problem is novel and unique and faces great resistance to change. Solving a wicked problem also requires a great number of people to change their mindsets and behavior. In other words, *the people seeking to solve the problem are also causing it.* The solution, in biblical language, requires radical conversion.[22]

Yes, these three dangers are massive challenges. A moral imagination helps us see that each of these crises is also rooted in our lives.

This requires a radical shift in how we think about change. As the writer, farmer, and environmental activist Wendell Berry puts it, "there is no public crisis that is not also private." Hope requires rebuilding what Berry calls "the integrity of private life." While we greatly need better government, "we also need better minds, better friendships, better marriages, better communities," says Berry. "We need persons and households that do not have to wait upon organizations, but can make necessary changes in themselves, on their own."[23]

Berry calls for a radical shift in how we think about deep change: "For most of the history of this country our motto, implied or spoken, has been Think Big. I have come to believe that a better motto, and an essential one now, is Think Little." Think Big imagines that someone else needs to change to solve the problem. But here is how those who Think Little are already solving the problem:

> A couple who make a good marriage, and raise healthy, morally competent children, are serving the world's future more directly and surely than any political leader,

though they never utter a public word. A good farmer who is dealing with the problem of soil erosion on an acre of ground has a sounder grasp of that problem and cares more about it and is probably doing more to solve it than any bureaucrat who is talking about it in general. A man who is willing to undertake the discipline and the difficulty of mending his own ways is worth more to the conservation movement than a hundred who are insisting merely that the government and the industries mend their ways.[24]

Political policies carry both indispensable power for good and unparalleled power for bad. Big approaches are required to face the unprecedented dangers of our day.

But equally important are the possibilities that become apparent to minds that are prepared to Think Little. The remedies that Think Little opens up are deep and difficult precisely because they "require a new kind of life—harder, more laborious," yet at the same time "richer in meaning and more abundant in real pleasure."

What Think Little remedies and new kind of life might we engage with respect to the three dangers?

People-to-people exchange between Americans and the Chinese. After thirty years of engaging China, Mennonite Partners in China (MPC) executive director Myrrl Byler is alarmed by recent years of increasing tensions between China and the United States. "It's the one place in the world," he says, "where the conflict could be the greatest, and we the church can't go missing."[25]

The moral imagination needed, Myrrl believes, is to put a human face on those being called "the enemy." MPC has done this through people-to-people exchange. MPC has brought over 300 Chinese visiting scholars to US schools, sent more than 300 English teachers to China from the United States and Canada, and facilitated service abroad opportunities for several dozen young adult Chinese. When MPC sent twenty US students to China, MPC took nine Chinese professors into the United States for the same amount of time. Byler states,

> We weren't just going to China to teach English, we're inviting you to come to our campuses to help us learn where you are coming from, exchanging knowledge on medicine, mental health, nursing, agriculture. We have worked from a theology of presence, of mutuality. That's the kind of long-term work that needs to be done again now. We need to re-engage with hope and excitement, to share life with those who are called our enemies.[26]

Actions of social peacemaking Byler describes plant seeds for a new future at a volatile global time. In that spirit, here are four ways to live the alternative in a bipolar, China-versus-US world.

Study Chinese language. China has at least 3,500 years of civilization before the Communist Party, and in general, Chinese people know far more about the United States than Americans know about China. While 400 million Chinese people are learning English and over 300,000 study in the United States, only 200,000 Americans are studying Chinese and only 20,000 studying in China. Chinese characters are endlessly fascinating, and their four-character idioms are packed with wisdom (three favorites: "When drinking water, don't forget the source." "To create problems for no reason." "Teacher for a day, father for a lifetime.").

Read books that show China's complexity. My personal favorites for learning about the ins and outs of today's China are the Inspector Chen novels by Qiu Xiaolong, about a poem-quoting, truth-seeking chief police inspector in Shanghai who investigates murders, rises above the corruption of the Party, and, with other people of goodwill, charts an alternative path.

Build relationships of mutual learning with Chinese students. One of the Deep Common Journey partners of our former church in North Carolina is International Students, Inc. ISI connects our church to many students studying at the many universities in the area. Those relationships interrupt the "danger of a single story" narratives of hostility and plant good seeds for a future of peace.

Join the Stop AAPI Hate movement. Rising animosity toward China inspires alarming bigotry and crimes against Asian and Pacific Island people in America. Get educated and support efforts to stop this.[27]

Spiritual disciplines and technology. Columnist Peggy Noonan sounded the alarm. "The nature and experience of childhood has been changed by social media in some very bad ways," she writes. "Why can't we, as a nation, change this?"[28] Here are some Think Little ways to be the change we seek for the nation.

Practice the spiritual discipline of nonviolent communication. When President Abraham Lincoln got angry with someone who angered or offended him, he often wrote what he called a "hot letter." Many of these letters were later discovered, marked by Lincoln as "never sent."[29] Today, with the power of algorithms, a single angry post can multiply outrage. To paraphrase Philippians 4:8-9: "Finally, brothers and sisters, whatever is true, whatever is noble, whatever is right, whatever is pure, whatever is lovely, whatever is admirable—if anything is excellent or praiseworthy—post about such things." As my Japanese pastor-friend Katsuki Hirano says, "Don't be afraid to be a minority." Communication becomes violent when the fear of losing control overtakes us. Means matter as much as ends. After writing a post about something that makes you angry, pray, wait twenty-four hours, then decide whether to hit "send."

Fast regularly from social media and screens. For a full month each year, a Korean friend of mine, who has a large social media presence, puts it completely aside. He calls it "fasting from flattery and from fury."

Organize a church group to study the relationship between Christian faith and the minerals in all the tech devices you use. Minerals extracted from countries such as the DRC create conflict and are a dirty secret of the technology industry. Some are guilty of this exploitation. But all of us benefit, and all are responsible. In your study, make the connections between cobalt, conflict, and Christianity, and consider actions the group can take in light of what you learn.

Making climate change personal. Think Little opens up immediate possibilities for everyday actions on behalf of a healthy environment. Here are two:

Create daily rhythms. On your way to starting a new church group to talk about climate change, why not, as Wendell Berry says, "pick up some cans and bottles yourself." On your way to meetings about antipollution policy with elected officials, "drive your car less, use less fuel in your home." As you click "yes" to join the Sierra Club, "turn off the lights you're not using." There may be no better personal involvement than gardening. The more we garden, in fact, the more our hands will be in God-given soil and the less they'll be scrolling.[30]

Talk about climate change with your family, friends, and church members. Katharine Hayhoe, a Canadian climate scientist and evangelical Christian, says studies show that only 8 percent of Americans are "dismissive" of climate change, and that many more who are considered "doubtful" can be swayed. "It's not about the loudest voices. It's about everyone else who doesn't understand why climate change matters or what they can do about it."[31] Hayhoe has some advice for opening up conversation. Because the term *climate change* is viewed by some as a liberal hoax, she avoids using the term with farmers, using "climate variability" and "long-term trends" instead. For one "climate doubter" named David Dale, talking about his favorite fishing hole with Hayhoe was a turning point. He said there were fewer and fewer fish, and algae was covering the lake. "That's what happens when the water gets warmer," Hayhoe said. "It breaks my heart," Dale told her. "That lake is finished."[32]

Like Dale, I was a latecomer to seeing why human-driven climate change matters.

You couldn't ignore the pollution in Seoul when I was growing up. But global warming was not in our vocabulary, and environmental activists, I admit, were written off as "tree huggers." In Mississippi, my housemates and I used the *More-with-Less Cookbook*, but that was about recipes, not a cause. When the city of Jackson distributed green recycling baskets, it didn't work—they quickly became handy laundry carriers and storage bins.

Back when we started the Center for Reconciliation at Duke Divinity School, our faculty colleague Norman Wirzba—a scholar on food and faith—once told me "You guys think reconciliation is only about people." He was right. I didn't see the connection to land, air, animals, plants.

But at the same time, I have always loved the natural world. Getting away from polluted Seoul to Daecheon Beach and its sand, ocean, pine trees, shells. Driving the Natchez Trace Parkway in Mississippi, passing forests of maple, oak, and hickory trees. The beaches of Emerald Isle in North Carolina, where the sight of a wave-surfing dolphin always takes my breath away. Fishing on Bristol Pond in Vermont, surrounded by pastoral landscape of farms and forests, where, whether or not my son and I land a bass, there is no such thing as a bad day. The Adirondack Mountains of upper-state New York and its lakes, pine trees, grass. My daughter rolls her eyes when I talk about my close canoe encounters with loons, that majestic diving water bird that has worked its way into my soul. I admit I didn't get birds until I married a birdwatcher. But Donna converted me, and every new sighting is a thrill. Over a lifetime of frantic activity and intensity, I don't know who I'd be without all the gifts these places and creatures have poured into me. Even writing these words my heart fills with joy.

Gradually, I began to see it: What would my life be without Daecheon, Emerald Isle, Bristol Pond, the Adirondacks, dolphins, loons, pine trees, being barefoot in sand and grass? And from there, what are similar places for others, and what is their world becoming when these gifts are disappearing for them? Especially when their entire livelihood depends on that land? And from there, what is the relationship between land, animals, plants, and human life?

Walking the woods recently in Vermont, I passed an owl high on a tree, looking down on me. Later an owl (the same one, I imagined) landed on the backyard birdfeeder and glared at me inside the back porch. I wondered, "Who is the host and who is the guest?" Passing a dog licking the face of her human companion, I now wonder, "Who is taking care of whom?"

In the words of Pope Francis, the world is, indeed, "our common home." I now see it: caring for creation is at the heart of God's work of shalom and reconciling all things.

Last year, for the first time, Donna and I sent what was for us a sizable donation to the Adirondack Council to support their advocacy work to protect the water, air, and wildlife of those mountains and lakes that have given our family so much joy.

In the face of the powers of dominion in this world, that action is very little. But through the journey that led to it, my moral imagination has been awakened. And when that shift happens for more and more of us, and we join in common cause, history can turn, and another reality becomes possible.

CHAPTER EIGHT

Renewing the Church for a World Longing for Hope

*We look at ourselves in this waiting moment—the kinds of people
we are. The questions persist: What are we doing with our lives?
What are the motives that order our days? What is the end of
our doings? Where are we trying to go? Where do we put the
emphasis and where are our values focused? For what end do we
make sacrifices? Where is my treasure and what do I love most
in life? What do I hate most in life and to what am I true?*

HOWARD THURMAN, *MEDITATIONS OF THE HEART*

Renewals need renewing.

Monasteries during the Dark Ages, the first Franciscans
facing a church weakened by wealth and power, the Protestant
Reformation alarmed by legalism and religious profiteering,
the early Anabaptists disturbed by a cozy relationship between
church and state, Methodism seeking to revive the staid
Church of England—all began as renewal movements in times
of historical crisis. All brought fresh air and life into the church
and world of their time.

But eventually, renewal is replaced by complacency, bureau-
cracy, decay, and mission drift. All renewals eventually need
renewing. And when personal faith and weekly church life

becomes predictable routine, or is turned upside down by crisis, it is true for our own lives as well.

As our pandemic era begins, distress signals are coming from many places in the church, all of which began as renewal movements.

From the Anglican Church in North America: Priest Kimberly Deckel began her pastoral ministry with optimism. She wasn't prepared for how, for many people, church was merely a place to hear an inspiring message, and for "the church" to "become synonymous with things like *abuse, legalism, hypocrisy,* and *racism,* causing many to hesitate to even walk through church doors."[1]

From a Catholic layperson: Ross Douthat, a *New York Times* columnist, lamented that "the leaders of my faith have—how to put this charitably—no clear idea what they're doing. They are in a difficult position, managing decline and transformation, but even judged by that gentle standard, they are failing."[2]

From the Southern Baptist Convention: In 2021, because sexual abuse and racism were not being addressed in its ranks, Russell Moore resigned from a leadership position in the denomination. "We now see young evangelicals walking away from evangelicalism not because they do not believe what the church teaches," he said at a conference, "but because they believe that the church itself does not believe what the church teaches."[3]

Distress signals are coming from Christians not only in the United States. Younger believers in South Korea often tell me that they believe the church there has not only lost the trust of Korean society but is often a source of social harm because of pastoral scandals, a gospel of personal prosperity and success, and a mean-spirited public presence. Many in the younger generation are leaving the church. When I was growing up in South Korea, churches were just beginning to grow. South Korea is on its way from being a country with a small minority of Christians, to a country dominated by Christianity in fast-growing churches and social power, to a post-Christian country—in just one generation.

From the United Methodist Church to the Anglican Communion to Mennonites, denominations are unraveling due to divisions. Church attendance has declined since the pandemic. Many people have dropped out completely and are not coming back, deciding that worship is not as important as they thought. The upheaval of our new time will permanently change the way people relate to church.

There are two kinds of time in New Testament Greek— *chronos* time and *kairos* time. *Chronos* is watch time, historical time, human time. *Kairos* is God's time, in Jesus' words "the time [*kairos*] has come . . . the kingdom of God has come near. Repent and believe the good news!" (Mark 1:15 NIV).

As we listen to this *chronos* time of church crisis in America and the world, what is the *kairos*? What word do we sense from God in these distress signals?

It is a time of unsettling for the church, of being unmade and remade. It is a time that has not only exposed great new challenges in the world but superficiality and decay in the church. And it has also exposed our idols.

It's not a coincidence that Jesus's anger was most fully on display in his cleansing of the temple, carrying a homemade whip as he turned over tables and railed against turning God's house into a house of profit (John 2:13-17). His greatest anger is reserved for the household of faith. God does not tolerate idolatry in the church. Yet so many of our congregations tolerate the idolatry of political partyism, of public success at the expense of private integrity, of zero-sum ethnic rivalry, of a personal prosperity that passes by the vulnerable at the side of the road.

Considering the distress signals, the decay, the idolatry of a church that does not believe what the church itself teaches, if I had to choose one word to name what I sense is happening with the church in our time, it is *pruning*. Without regular pruning, a fruit tree will gradually lose health and vigor, and its fruit will lose its quality. Pruning is painful. It requires trimming, cutting off, losing limbs that we are used to having and that seem precious. And pruning does not have immediate effect. After a tree is pruned it looks . . . well, a bit small, modest, humble. But in time—just wait—better and more fruit is coming.

Here's what pruning looked like for Emerywood Baptist Church in High Point, North Carolina. Due to pandemic difficulties, Timothy Peoples, the black pastor of this multiracial congregation, hit a breaking point. People also left the church. Yet others became more vulnerable and open, and faced their privileges, and surrounded Peoples with support. "The pandemic shutdown was actually really good for us," said Peoples. "We finally took on hard discussions and challenges that we had been putting off for so long."[4]

Renewals need renewing. The pruning of the church itself, and the good fruit God makes of it, is precisely what the world longs for.

Part of that pruning in our new time relates to Jesus' call, "Repent and believe the good news." How do we carry that call into encounters with people of other faiths and people of no faith? How do we plant new churches where believers are few?

Yet I propose that a more important question comes first. Listening to the distress signals in the church, the question is, *What kind of Christianity are we evangelizing people into?*

In the Gospel of John, with his disciples the night before his death, Jesus prayed to his Holy Father for those who would believe in him through the message of his disciples, asking, "that they may be one as We are one—I in them and You in Me—that they may be perfectly united, so that the world may know that You sent Me and have loved them just as You have loved Me" (John 1:22 BSB).

According to Jesus, the church's quality of life, its unity, is the sign that it is filled with the love of Christ and that Jesus is Lord. But when that quality of life becomes infected, then the words of my mentor John Perkins become very prophetic: "We have overevangelized the world too lightly."

The promises of Western modernity are now running on empty. As David Brooks writes, "The age of the autonomous individual, the age of the narcissistic self, the age of consumerism and moral drift has left us with bitterness and division, a surging mental health crisis and people just being nasty to one another." Brooks is convinced that millions of people are looking for an alternative, "some system of belief that is communal, that gives life transcendent meaning."[5]

What an opportunity for the renewal of the church. I want to propose six essentials for renewing the church in this new era in our world: our destination, formation, congregations, mission, identity, and intimacy.

A BOLD DESTINATION

Some Christians say, "Let's not focus on what we believe but what we do. Theology divides. Action unites people and changes the world." Does service unite and theology divide? I put this question once to Stanley Hauerwas, who answered, "But how would you know what to do?" Unless guided by the prayer Jesus taught his disciples, for example, how would we know that we are called to ask God to forgive us as we forgive those who sin against us (Matthew 6:9-13)? Forgiving is hardly our first human impulse.

When Christianity becomes poisoned by racial superiority, hypocrisy, attachment to partisan power, or a gospel of individual enrichment, it raises questions: How do we know what to do? What story of Christianity are we evangelizing people into?

When a friend of mine turned sixty, she received a birthday card. On the front was a picture of a woman with white hair driving a car, with the words, "At our age, what good is a GPS if we can't remember why we got in the car in the first place?"

The first question facing the renewal of the church is not What should we do? The first question is, Why are we in the car, and what's our destination?

Scripture tells a story of the larger drama in which our lives play a part, a story that provides us a destination worth sacrificing for, a story of hope and healing that this world desperately longs for. The short version goes like this:

> From now on, therefore, we regard no one from a human point of view. . . . So if anyone is in Christ, there is a new creation: everything old has passed away; see, everything has become new! All this is from God, who reconciled us to himself though Christ, and has given us the ministry of reconciliation; that is, in Christ God was reconciling the world to himself, not counting their trespasses against them, and entrusting the message of reconciliation to us. So we are ambassadors for Christ, since God is making his appeal through us; we entreat you on behalf of Christ, be reconciled to God. (2 Corinthians 5:16–20 NRSVue)

Several crucial truths emerge from this story:

The destination toward which God is taking the world is reconciliation. And that reconciliation is God's initiative, restoring the world to God's intentions. Healing the world doesn't begin with us and our strategies. Reconciliation is a gift, participation with what God is already doing with the gifts God provides.

God reconciled the world to himself, not just individuals. The scope of God's reconciliation is personal and political, spiritual and social, material and cosmic.

The message of reconciliation is far more radical and beautiful than a call to humanitarian tolerance. God's new creation is a whole new dimension, a way of thinking and living that is different from our cultural assumptions.

Reconciliation is not a theory, technique, or achievement. It is a journey. And this journey has not been entrusted to professionals and specialists. Reconciliation's ambassadors are "anyone in Christ": everyday people. It is the ministry of the whole church.

Reconciliation is both "already" and "not yet." The change is real and happening, but also yet to be fulfilled, for "the old" resists. Reconciliation is God's call to conversion into the way of Christ, a profound turning from an old place to a new place.

To what destination does this story take us?

Dr. Martin Luther King Jr. offered an answer to a world longing for hope. In 1956, he was speaking in a church in Montgomery, Alabama. The occasion marked one year of an economic boycott in the city to bring pressure to change racist policies. Much had been achieved, including legal victories and ordinary people of faith growing in nonviolent character and public resistance.

But as their appointed leader, King wanted to be sure everyone knew why they were in the vehicle and where they were headed. He wanted to lift their eyes beyond the immediate crisis to set their eyes on the horizon.

"It is true that as we struggle for freedom we will have to boycott at times," said King. Montgomery was a city in the grip of racial injustice and white supremacy. For liberation to happen, boycotts and legal campaigns were necessary. But that, said King, was not the ultimate destination. "But we remember that as we boycott, the boycott is not an end within itself. . . . [The] end is reconciliation; the end is redemption; the end is the creation of the beloved community."[6]

The destination of the beloved community is essential for our time as well. As Vinoth Ramachandra writes, "King's political discourse envisioned the regeneration of the nation as a whole." The beloved community was "a reconciliation that went beyond justice for his own people without bypassing it. While confronting the guilt of white oppression and repentance were necessary, the healing of relationships was the ultimate goal." King's vision of the beloved community embraced not only those working for freedom but those working against it, including a white Christian population that had lost their foundational DNA.[7]

When Richard Hays was dean of Duke Divinity School, he said, "This school should not have a center for reconciliation—it should be a center for reconciliation." Beloved community provides us a way of fighting the evils in the world and the church in a way that doesn't transform us into what we fight. The destination of beloved community directs our sights beyond partisan politics to a broader vision of transformation.

REFORMING FORMATION

The second essential for renewing the church is formation that brings deep change in our lives.

I am moved every time I visit the 9/11 memorial in New York City—the footprints of the twin World Trade Center towers that fell now filled with two memorials of flowing water. It is a peaceful place to remember and mourn. I also feel the gravity of the attack. Before 9/11, no one imagined such an assault—terrorists training in US flight schools, boarding planes as passengers, taking them over, flying them as missiles, the towers falling. And the deadly response from the US military—war in Iraq, then in Afghanistan.

It requires serious forethought and formation to create both a terrorist and a soldier, skillfully trained in heart, mind, and body to kill for a cause they believe in.

Next to the impact of that formation, Christianity can often look like a weak culture offering a weak response to the challenges of our times. The way a Rwandan bishop once put it to me was "How do we form Christians for whom the waters of baptism flow stronger than the blood of tribalism?"

Looking at the crises facing the church, pastor and author Tim Keller names the seriousness of the task: "We need to really redo Christian education. Completely."[8]

One person taking this seriously is Walter Kim, installed in 2019 as director of the National Association of Evangelicals, which is composed of forty denominations. A Korean American leader, Kim said his first priority was "grappling with the issue of racial justice and reconciliation." His next priority was "public discipleship."

While Kim believes evangelical churches know how to do premarital and marital counseling, "I'd love to see similar programs for the church's ability to equip people in their public and civic engagement." Equipping evangelicals to separate truth from propaganda, prophetic speech from poisonous communication, political partisanship from faithful public engagement—this is desperately needed. Kim said evangelicals can learn much from the black church, which "understood their church couldn't just address personal transformation but also their place in society."[9]

I helped give birth to institutes on three different continents that form Christian leaders in the ministry of justice and reconciliation—the Duke Summer Institute for Reconciliation in the United States, the African Great Lakes Institute, and the Christian Forum for Reconciliation in Northeast Asia. Each became a "school of conversion" in which people are deeply changed. But serious formation requires serious pedagogy (our methods of teaching and learning). Formation requires time—the institutes are not one or two days but five days. Formation is not only what we study but who we study with—across divides, we reflect on Scripture and share our stories. Formation is multisensory and interdisciplinary—daily rhythms of worship, teaching from both scholars and practitioners, eating together, seminars, pilgrimages that relocate bodies to strange places.

To divorce Christianity from sexual abuse and partisan political power, to form border-crossing people, and to experience racial healing require schools of conversion. We must completely reform Christian formation.

HEALTHY CONGREGATIONAL LIFE

The third essential for renewing the church for the new time in our world is each of us going deep in a local congregation, contributing to its health.

"On this rock I will build my church," said Jesus (Matthew 16:18). *My church.* Not my nonprofit organization. Not my private time of prayer. Not my campaign for a righteous cause. The story of Acts is the story of small, fragile congregations being formed, physically gathering to worship the crucified and risen Lord in towns and cities. In Christian theology and practice, congregations are nonnegotiable for Christian life. There simply is no substitute for being part of a congregation.

First, healthy congregations remind us that we are all human creatures—limited, all dependent on God, and as such, beloved.

"It's a wonderfully ordinary path, being a churchgoing Christian," reflects editor and writer Sheryl Fullerton. "Sometimes it's boring. Sometimes it's thrilling. Sometimes I feel completely plugged in, surrounded by love and spirit. Sometimes it makes me cry because I am so moved. Other times it's a little empty, and it feels like the most interesting thing going on is the mysterious ruffling of Deidre Washington's hairdo."[10] Over time, as this ordinariness blends with prayer, praise, preaching, Scripture, and life together, creatureliness becomes inseparable from holiness.

Second, in healthy congregational life we receive other very different bodies that make up the body of Christ.

"Christians need to hear the babies crying in church. They need to see the reddened eyes of a friend across the aisle," Collin Hansen wrote in a *New York Times* essay about online church. "They need to chat with the recovering drug addict who shows up early but still sits in the back row. They need to taste the bread and wine. They need to feel the choir crescendo toward the assurance of hope in what our senses can't yet perceive."[11]

Through the proximity of different bodies together in worship, together hearing, seeing, chatting, tasting, singing, feeling, others lead us to Christ in very unexpected ways.

Third, congregations form us to understand that renewal in our lives and congregations is not a matter of cause-and-effect efficiency. As Pope Francis once said, the church is not an NGO—"it's a love story."[12] Healthy congregations are not slick and the results are not obvious. A congregation doesn't hire their members or fire them (though we might sometimes wish it otherwise). It's a coalition of the willing, warts and all. Every church I joined I dearly loved and they regularly drove me nuts.

Fourth, healthy congregations put ministry over metrics. While "numbers matter, they don't define us," writes California pastor Karl Vaters, who keeps a list of nonnumerical criteria to determine his congregation's health. The list runs from "It's a good place to ask hard questions," to "People like bringing their friends," to "People are more excited about the future than the past."[13]

Here are two criteria I would add: First, people have a relationship with vulnerable communities in the area—they know specific people and are involved with specific churches and organizations. Second, people are comfortable sharing church life with people who make them feel uncomfortable. In her church, Anglican pastor Tish Harrison Warren says that people in their early twenties testify over and over that "one of the hardest and best things about church was that they had to sit with people of different ages, classes, and political beliefs. It was a practice they found inconvenient, yes, but truly grounding, nourishing and good."[14]

A healthy congregation also nourishes its pastors, supporting their unique vocation and the heavy load they carry.

During our North Carolina years, our pastor was Rev. Allan Poole. While I love congregational life, I don't have the patience to be a pastor. But Allan delighted in pastoral details. While he is a very gifted communicator, at the coffee shop he and I frequented, I often saw him with a parishioner. Invariably, Allan was the one doing most of the listening. When we arrived in Durham, our church celebrated Holy Communion once a month. Becoming friends, I learned how Allan longed for this essential Christian sacrament to be offered weekly. Serving as an elder, I watched him lead the way toward change. But Allan believed the move should have unanimous support. He patiently prodded us forward—and it took a full decade. Every week after that, I couldn't wait to walk forward, hold out my hands, look into Allan's eyes, and hear his words, "the body of Christ, broken for you."

One time Allan and I went to a retreat center where silence was practiced in all public spaces. During meals, I got my plate, went to my seat, and got down to business. Meanwhile Allan was quietly being attentive to the other strangers who were guests, using hand motions to ask if he could pour a cup of water, offering utensils, giving a smiling nod of acknowledgment. Noticing people. Serving people. At the end of the retreat, we ran into another guest who said to Allan, "I heard you're a pastor. I just knew you were!"

No, the beloved shepherd was not me. Thank God for those who are otherwise. Renewal depends on doing all we can to ensure our pastors are given space and time to be refreshed in their indispensable calling.

NEW WINESKINS OF MISSION

The fourth essential for renewing the church in these times is creating new wineskins to carry out God's crosscultural mission in a world where Christian vitality has shifted geographically and culturally.

The new wine of hope cannot be sustained without new wineskins. "No one pours new wine into old wineskins," said Jesus. "No, new wine must be poured into new wineskins" (Luke 5:37-38 NIV). Wineskins are made of leathered animal skin. Old wineskins become brittle and can burst as fresh wine ferments in them.

Throughout Christian history, creative and unprecedented new structures have been crafted to ferment renewal movements. The monastery, the hospital, the voluntary society— these were all Christian social innovations that renewed the church and brought fresh gifts to our neighbors in the world.

Now new wineskins are needed to ferment the church's border-crossing mission. Although Christianity's vitality has shifted from North America and Europe to Latin America, Africa, and Asia, white American believers institutionalized a way of engaging the world that needs radical reform. As discussed in chapter five, the problem is the establishment of one-way traffic.

According to Andrew Walls, the great historian of Christian mission, the origin of one-way traffic is England's eighteenth-century Protestant independent agencies, or "voluntary societies," which raised their own money and staff and sent those Western resources to other countries. When it comes to one-way giving and sending, this model was extremely effective. As Walls explains:

> The Protestant missionary movement developed by means of the voluntary society, and America perfected its application to the purposes of overseas mission. The resultant

mission agencies were admirably designed for their task: to direct the resources of Christians in one country to the preaching of the gospel and the establishing of churches in another country. That is, the task in hand was principally giving; the design was essentially for one-way traffic.[15]

But "with the new shape of the Christian world," wrote Walls, "there are needs for which the perfect instrument was not designed. Instruments are now needed for *two*-way traffic: for sharing and for receiving."[16]

I would go further than Walls: two-way traffic of sharing and receiving is what was *always* needed, it is the gospel norm, and—while there are remarkable exceptions—centuries of mostly one-way traffic have impoverished Western Christianity and created institutional captivities of paternalism and dominance by white leaders. Without innovative new structures that can stretch to those who have been left out, our Christian institutions are limiting their maturity into Christlikeness. As Walls puts it, "The very height of Christ's full stature (Eph. 4:13) is reached only by the coming together of the different cultural entities into the body of Christ. Only 'together,' not on our own, can we reach his full stature."[17]

The organization I know that comes the closest to being a new wineskin of two-way traffic is InterVarsity Christian Fellowship.[18] Over its eighty-year history InterVarsity has matured from being a white-dominated organization to become a profoundly crosscultural and transnational community. Their decisions along the way are indicative of the sacrifices required to make renewal possible.

In 1991 the University of California, Berkeley, became a university without an ethnic majority. "We had to ask what God was doing in the world," said then–InterVarsity president Steve Hayner. "And if God was moving to the Southern Hemisphere and changing color in leadership, we had to reflect that."

InterVarsity decided to carry out two very different models at the same time, some campus chapters being intentionally ethnic-specific (focused on African American tradition, or Asian American tradition, for example) and some intentionally multiethnic. Each model was seen as offering unique gifts on a complex racial landscape whereby "multiethnic" often became the de facto control of white culture and power.

InterVarsity addressed power imbalances by dedicating significant financial resources to assist ethnic-minority staff in raising support and rising in leadership. For some white students unaccustomed to sharing power, the journey could be difficult. As more campus chapters became multiethnic, more white students left InterVarsity to join other campus groups. Still, cross-racial friendships were common, another unique characteristic of the InterVarsity approach.

Hayner said he often turned to Scripture to refute accusations that InterVarsity was simply being politically correct, pointing to the Holy Spirit driving the church in mission across cultures in the book of Acts. "This is not just a casual theme in Scripture," Hayner said. Being grounded in a biblical vision gave leaders courage to keep taking risks, believing that Inter-Varsity was becoming more complete in Christ along the way.

Over the decades, multiethnic mission moved from being nonexistent, to marginal, to mainstream. Along the way were dramatic policy shifts about campus ministry, staff hiring, fundraising, and governance. InterVarsity became willing to pay a higher and higher price in order to gain a new reality, including losing alienated donors and board members.

According to Hayner, "IVCF is very self-reflective. They are constantly asking a series of questions about how are we doing, what's going on here. So they become reflective of money, structure, things that really reflect whether you're doing things well." He confessed how hard this is, slowing down decisions. Yet the underlying logic is what Hayner describes as InterVarsity's "theory of change": a commitment to Jesus' lordship, mediated by Scripture. This has included a capacity for self-criticism by creating public platforms for outside prophetic voices.[19]

In 2016, Tom Lin, a Taiwanese American, became the organization's first nonwhite president. InterVarsity is a story of a renewal being renewed.

If the voluntary society was as revolutionary for the reformulation of Christian life and mission as the monasteries were in their own time, a new historical challenge of "sharing and receiving" requires new instruments, writes Walls, that "may prove equally disturbing."[20] What first disturbed InterVarsity led to great fruitfulness, demonstrating that new wineskins for a new era of crosscultural and transnational Christianity is possible.

AMBASSADORS IN THE PUBLIC SQUARE

The fifth essential for renewing the church for our new pandemic-era world is a positive, world-engaging identity and way of being.

For too long, a Christian lust for social control has become too close an allegiance—on both Right and Left—with political power and national values. In response, there have been calls in recent years for Christians to step away from society and its infections. Our world surely needs congregations and monastic-type communities that faithfully live an alternative way of life in a world that often resists the way of Christ. They are an indispensable gift to society, proving that another way is possible and bringing light into the darkness.

At the same time, this often comes with an oppositional stance and too much distance from the complexities of culture and society. The church's main public task—forming Christians who are faithful disciples—is by no means our only public task. To address the challenges in this book, living an alternative is not adequate.

I propose that renewing the church of this pandemic era calls us to embrace an ambassador identity given to us in two of Paul's letters. In 2 Corinthians, he writes that God "has committed to us the message of reconciliation. We are therefore Christ's ambassadors, as though God were making his appeal through us" (5:19-20 NIV). Then, in Ephesians: "Pray also for me, that whenever I speak, words may be given me so that I will fearlessly make known the mystery of the gospel, for which I am an ambassador in chains. Pray that I may declare it fearlessly, as I should" (6:19-20).

Used by Paul, *ambassador* is a positive, culture-engaging term. Ambassadors are representatives of another country who are publicly visible and active in the country where they are sent.

But ambassadors of Christ do this very differently from ambassadors of a country. Those ambassadors have high rank, privilege, and status. They travel in the back seat of a black bulletproof car with a driver and security team. They can flee the country when things get risky. They have immunity without local accountability.

Ambassadors of Christ do not follow the way of immunity but the way of incarnation. Like their leader, they are present both to the broken and to the powerful. All of Christ's followers are called to be ambassadors. It is not privilege or status that qualifies you, but markers the Lord called "blessed"—poor in spirit, pure in heart, meek ones who mourn and are merciful, who thirst for justice and make peace. As Paul writes, "But we have this treasure in jars of clay, to show that the surpassing power belongs to God and not to us" (2 Corinthians 4:7).

If ambassadors are only oppositional in engaging the wider society, they are ineffective. While they represent a different kingdom and its values, they also develop a deep empathy with and appreciation for the place where they serve. Ambassadors both create a distinct culture and care for their common home with all humanity, crossing borders and creating intersections between the two.

Country ambassadors are limited by national interest. They are sent and don't stay long enough to be transformed by the places where they serve. But Christ's ambassadors both share and receive, and they report to, represent, and give allegiance to a foreign kingdom beyond the places where they live and serve. They are not messengers of national interest but of the destination of reconciliation given in 2 Corinthians 5:17-20.

Being ambassadors of Christ guides us as toward neither private religion nor political control, neither creating a Christian ghetto nor selling our souls to a governmental leader. We are ambassadors of Christ, not a country. Our leader sends us out with a diplomatic mission of reconciliation, with Christ appealing not only through our words but literally "through us" (2 Corinthians 5:20), through the quality of our very lives. That mission propels us into the public square to defend truth, justice, and mercy. It will be costly. It will put some of us in chains. But much is at stake for our world: making known the good news of reconciliation.[21]

Seeking the purity of the church while sacrificing public engagement can easily become another form of cultural mediocrity. The church of this new era will be renewed not only by being the church but by being ambassadors in society, actively engaged with the people, politics, economics, and cultures of this world.

INTIMACY WITH CHRIST

The final essential for renewing the church for this new time in our world is being rooted in the living Christ.

The twentieth-century missionary movement from mainline US churches had a profound global impact. But historian Robert Westbrook contends that these very missionaries ushered in a "post-Protestant America" as they returned to the United States and "attacked the paternalist presumptions of missionary preaching, expressed deep respect for the cultures and religions of the non-Western world, and placed humanitarian service above evangelization." While some strong critiques were needed, a problem resulted: "Ecumenical Protestants found it increasingly difficult thereafter . . . to say *what exactly Christianity brought to the missionary table that could not be found just as well in secular humanitarianism.*"[22]

A kind of spirituality or social action that does not need Christ cannot renew the church. A colleague at a respected evangelical organization once told me, "We send many young people to serve in poor communities. And often they come back more committed to justice but less committed to Jesus."

Jesus without justice, justice without Jesus—for the church, they are two sides of the same cheap coin of idolatry. If Christian life is reduced to social justice and humanitarianism, or to personal piety, then the living, liberating Christ no longer matters. A kind of Christianity that no longer needs the power of Christ cannot renew the church.

An icon sits on my desk. It was a gift from a Korean member of the Taizé community in France who led worship one year at our Christian Forum for Reconciliation in Northeast Asia. The gift is an image of the original icon, found in the remains of a monastery in Egypt and dated to the fifth century. It hangs today in the Louvre Museum in Paris. It is a painting on wood, and very small.

Some icons present Jesus as prophet—hand raised to speak. In others, Jesus is priest—clothed as a bishop, sitting on a big chair. And in others, Jesus is King of kings, crowned and seated on an ornate throne.

But this icon is strikingly different. The background is an ordinary rural setting of hills, sky, and earth. Jesus stands on a road, wearing an ordinary robe. Most of all, Jesus is not alone. At his side is another person, and Jesus' arm is raised not to speak but to embrace his companion. Taizé calls this icon *Christ and His Friend*.

It is often understood that Jesus performed three offices in his earthly ministry: Prophet, Priest, King. But this three-fold office of Christ misses something.

It misses Jesus in his last night with his disciples before his death, when Jesus washes their feet and says these words: "No longer do I call you servants, for the servant does not know what his master is doing; but I have called you friends, for all that I have heard from my Father I have made known to you" (John 15:15).

Christ and His Friend is an icon of intimacy. Their mouths are closed. But the friend has big ears. And in an easily missed nuance, they each have one eye on each other, and one eye on the road ahead. The friendship between Christ and companion is not closed, but open to the world. Christ holds the Scriptures—a hefty book. But the friend also holds something, a small scroll. We carry only one small part of the bigger story Christ holds. But we too have something to share.

As for me, I wouldn't have bothered with this long and difficult journey of Christian life, and all the ups and downs and "why bother" moments, without sensing Jesus walking with me, arm around me as friend. The one whom I believe whispers that I am beloved without doing anything.

Regarding the destination of reconciliation given in 2 Corinthians 5, a few sentences earlier Paul writes, "For Christ's love compels us" (2 Corinthians 5:14 NIV). What compels us forward is not our love for Christ, but Christ's love for us and for this world. The love of Christ—the one who was in the beginning with God, the one who calls us friends—that is the primary reality of the universe.

That is who walks with us to face the great challenges of our time. There is no renewal without Jesus as friend.

"I am the vine; you are the branches. If you remain in me and I in you, you will bear much fruit; apart from me you can do nothing" (John 15:5 NIV). It is the time of pruning. Don't be afraid. Don't be afraid to be more of a minority. For churches to get smaller. To lose political power. To face the decay and the idols. Receive the pruning of God's gentle hand. It's the only way for more, and better, fruit to come.

Rest for Restless Hearts

"On the Resurrection of the Body"

Without that beloved singular one,
Who would I be?
With each death, a part of my body departed,
Life suddenly after never the same:
Ripped away, irreplaceable, always, right there,
An absence for that one only.
Yet sometimes, seemingly in solitude,
I find one of them (or more) in my presence,
Feeling very words they would say,
With what look, tone, touch.
And I remember terrains of growth since each after,
As if their essence was forever grafted into the now:
Left behind,
Yet joined, and living.

I wrote this poem about all the people I've been close to who died too soon. Each loss was a crisis that shook me. Each a before and after in my life. Each was followed by a search for meaning and recovery. Each opened up difficult new unknowns.

Yet the title is "On the Resurrection of the Body." Their bodies and their lives mattered and still matter. And, I believe, they are still somehow present to this world. I still grieve losing them. Yet I also feel their power and presence—"as if forever grafted into the now." And I believe that is not disconnected from the terrains of growth since each "after."

A crisis hits our life, our loved ones, our world, and suddenly after life is never the same. But terrains of growth can also come after each "after." Indeed, our world is being shaken by many crises now. Our world longs to be renewed. And I hope that you, like me, long for renewal in your own life.

In this book I have tried to show that what God has done for the world, in Christ, enables Christian discipleship to provide a compelling response to the great challenges of our new time. What will happen if you engage the challenges and pursue the practices of renewal in this book?

As told in the book of Acts, Saul, the persecutor of the first Christians, was shaken by a crisis after he was confronted by the voice of Jesus on the Damascus Road (Acts 9:1-6). But in his letter to the church at Ephesus, Paul (formerly Saul) says that during that crisis, a revelation came to him "that through the gospel the Gentiles are heirs together with Israel, members together of one body, and sharers together in the promise in Christ Jesus" (Ephesians 3:3, 6 NIV). It was a new, earth-shaking idea in the world at the time, and the revelation given to Paul gave birth to a new reality of hope in society: communities of Gentiles and Jews sharing life together as one. As strangers who had been separated and alienated from each other, that new reality threw all of them, including Paul, onto unfamiliar and difficult ground. They had to learn new practices of worship, relationship, economic sharing, and mission. It wasn't easy. But as they learned new practices, their lives were profoundly changed, and they shed fresh light and hope into the society around them.

Reflecting on these transformations, Paul said God will do "immeasurably more than all we ask or imagine" (Ephesians 3:20 NIV). In challenging times, when we allow our lives to be interrupted by new truth from God, when we expose and resist idols in our hearts and communities, when we dare to walk onto unfamiliar and difficult ground, when we learn to practice a better, more beautiful, truer way of life, that's what happens in us and around us: immeasurably more than we ask or imagine.

Following that pattern of renewal and witness, with the challenges and practices in this book in mind, here are a few final words to guide and encourage you.

Step onto unfamiliar ground. This book's pathways will take you into new territory. Remember that, as with the church crossing the Gentile–Jewish divide in Acts, it is often only on strange and difficult ground that certain deep growth can come to our lives and world, whether that new terrain is internal or external, spiritual or social, relational or political. That's where strange ground becomes holy ground. Stepping from the known into the unknown can bring enormous growth in our lives. Pick one or two of the challenges and practices in this book that speak most deeply to you, think about what unfamiliar ground you can go into, and take a step of risk. I believe you will find God waiting for you there.

Seek restless companions. From big to little, the transformative adventures I've experienced have all been birthed in communities of the restless, people longing for a better and more beautiful way. Start by asking not who opposes you but who is restless. That's where creativity is ignited, and courage found. Facing great challenges, we need companions who make us better and help keep us going. Whether your campus, church, workplace, or town, look for and build a nucleus of people who are restless together. And remember that, like the communities Paul built between Gentiles and Jews, it is in a new *We* that we become a new Me and where innovation is released— build a community of the restless across walls and barriers.

Expect revelation. As it did with Paul, a crisis can become a time of profound revelation in our lives, a time that opens us up to see a new truth. God will not leave us alone and gives us everything we need to live in this challenging world. All the practices in this book grew out of crucibles of crisis; they change lives deeply and make the world better and more beautiful. Even more, they are gifts of God and, I dare say, means of grace. They are infused with the way of Jesus, and when we practice them, we are participating with Christ. When we dare to follow the ways of Jesus, as Paul says, we will receive "immeasurably more than we ask or imagine." Expect it! Watch for it!

Expect to find rest for your heart and soul. "Take my yoke upon you . . . for I am gentle and humble in heart, and you will find rest for your souls," said Jesus (Matthew 11:29 NIV). When you think about the challenges in this book, when you think about Jesus calling his followers to die to self, bear a cross, and be ambassadors of renewal in such a difficult time in our world, it seems strange to see how that "yoke" brings rest. But in his *Confessions*, writing to God, Augustine said, "you have made us for yourself, and our hearts are restless until they find their rest in you."

In the challenging new times in our world, if your heart is restless, living out practices of hope leads toward rest for your soul. Expect to see something better and more beautiful. Expect renewal. Expect immeasurably more than you ask or imagine.

Acknowledgments

This book was written during the strangest and most isolated period of my life, in a new city during the pandemic, when I was stripped of things that normally bring joy, communion, and inspiration. But many precious gifts came in the writing journey.

What a privilege, serving with my colleagues in Mennonite Central Committee across the world. They inspire me every day and show that it's possible for an organization to have integrity, humility, mutuality, and sacrifice at its very core.

In monthly calls with my friends Katsuki Hirano and Jongho Kim, we opened our hearts and lives to one another. Our friendship between Tokyo, Seoul, and New York was a lifeline. To two "pandemic friends," our elders Renie and Bill McCutchen: your hospitality and the fun times and deep conversations we shared sparked so much joy.

Al Hsu, my editor at InterVarsity Press, has been a great encourager and adviser. I can't say enough about my respect for IVP as a publisher over the years. During days writing in Lincoln, Vermont, never have I been so close to the natural world. A big shout out to my companion chickadees, wrens, owls, turkeys, porcupine, fox, bears (a little too close a couple times), deer—and even you relentless bird feeder-raiding chipmunks—who kept entertaining me with your wonders.

In the past four years I lost both of my parents, and life is not the same. Yet they continue to inspire me through the imprint of their constant humor, love of life, and joy in people.

One unexpected gift of the pandemic was getting closer with my brother, Mark. I'm so grateful for the friendship and deep conversations, and that magical trip to the Adirondacks.

Benjamin, Talia, and Christopher, my dear children, you blessed me with your humor, resilience, and support. What a pleasure to watch you grow and now speak wisdom to me.

I have dedicated this book to Donna—my soulmate and steadfast companion over thirty-five years of marriage. You amaze me and transform me through your gentle courage, faith, and calm. What a blessing, together sharing the adventure of New York City and its riches of culture, beauty, and dynamism. When I lost belief, you kept believing in me, kept encouraging, kept saying "all shall be well."

"The wilderness will lead you, to your heart, where I will speak" says the song "Hosea," which spoke to me constantly. I am filled with gratitude and wonder, Lord, that I still hear you speak, and that your mercies are still new every morning.

Questions for Reflection and Discussion

INTRODUCTION: RENEWING A SHAKEN WORLD

1. In what ways has this time of crisis been a before-and-after moment for you or your community (church, school, workplace, etc.)?
2. How do you understand the word *renewal*? What is the difference between learning and being renewed?
3. Have you ever experienced renewal in your life or community?
4. What does the author mean by the "pandemic x-ray"? What do you think the x-ray revealed?
5. The author writes, "We don't learn from experience, but from reflection on experience." Do you agree?
6. When have you experienced a crisis that turned into an opportunity?

1. BEARING JOY FOR A WORLD OF FRANTIC ANXIETY

1. What signs of increasing anxiety, stress, or burnout do you see in your community?
2. What is the difference between joy and what the author calls "excess positivity"? Why does the difference matter?
3. "Facing the crisis of a century and our opportunity for renewal, I believe the most essential virtue is joy." What

does the author mean? Does that resonate with you? What do you think is the most essential virtue?

4. Are there practices or relationships that spark or create space for joy in your life? Give an example and describe its impact on you.

5. There are far more biblical passages about *God's* love for us and the world than about *our* love for God or our neighbor. What are the implications of this for your life?

6. What is the difference between a culture of demands and a culture of grace? Can you give an example of one or the other?

7. Read Luke 10:25-42. What does it mean to bring these two stories together—the Jericho Road and Bethany?

8. "God's response to burnout is belovedness." What does the author mean? What might that look like in places of burnout?

2. CENTERING THE VULNERABLE FOR A WORLD OF RISING DISPARITY

1. "The vulnerable are at the center of God's action for the world in Jesus Christ." Who are the vulnerable in the communities where you live? Do you see a group that is in danger of being written off as "useless"?

2. Of the five actions of the Samaritan described in this chapter, which is most challenging for you? Why?

3. In what place would it be most unsettling for you to engage vulnerable people?

4. What is the "Jericho Road" in the context where you live?

5. If there are some things God can only teach us by relocating our bodies onto strange ground, what might that strange ground be for you or your church?

6. "Privilege is a form of power that makes us blind to what is blindingly obvious to those who lack that privilege." What do you think about that statement?

7. Can you think of examples of the benevolence model in your community? How does the benevolence model hinder us from knowing Christ more deeply? Which practice in this chapter provides a way to move beyond that approach, and what would it look like to implement it?

3. BEING PEACEMAKERS FOR A WORLD OF SURGING POLARIZATION

1. Can you give an example of a "single story" you might have about another group?

2. The author describes a healthy tension between not being silent about injustice and being bridges between alienated groups. What is the difference between the two approaches? Can you think of an example where this tension exists?

3. What "We markers" does the author name? What are yours?

4. What did you take away from the story about the author and Katsuki Hirano? How were people in this chapter impoverished by not expanding their *We*? Has someone or some experience interrupted a "single story" you held? What was the change?

5. What is the difference between oppositional thinking and opposable thinking? Give an example in which opposable thinking is helpful.

6. What makes restorative justice different from other types of justice?

7. Have you ever experienced or seen how "love without truth lies" or "truth without love kills"?

8. Where might you be called to expand your *We*? How could that be a step toward knowing Christ more deeply?

4. REDEEMING POWER FOR A WORLD OF POLITICAL MEDIOCRITY

1. Share your thoughts on this sentence: "If the church is not talking about politics it is not the church."

2. Can you think of examples of political power providing an indispensable good? How about political power being an unparalleled danger? In those situations, how did Christians respond?

3. Reflecting on the story of Barbara Jordan, can you think of any just politicians? What qualities do/did they have?

4. "The practice of politics is the use of political power for love of neighbor, just relationships, and the flourishing of life in common." How does that definition of politics differ from how people normally think of politics? By that definition, how has the use of politics been twisted in our time?

5. What does the author mean by political mediocrity?

6. When is compromise good and when is it a problem?

7. Have you ever experienced or witnessed the problem of partyism? What was the impact? How can partyism become a form of idolatry for the church?

8. Do you come from a faith tradition that prefers access to political power or distance from political power? How has this influenced you regarding maintaining a healthy balance?

9. After reading this chapter, has it changed your views on why redeeming political power is critical for Christian discipleship? If so, how?

10. To address political mediocrity, which action steps do you need to prioritize in your life, community, or church? What would it look like to put them into practice?

5. MAKING TRANSNATIONAL DISCIPLES FOR A WORLD OF AMERICAN BLINDERS

1. Do you agree that Christian DNA is transnational? What does this imply for our lives?

2. The author writes, "When we are blind to American privilege, it prevents us from seeing our neighbor outside America and what it means to love that neighbor." What examples have you seen of this happening?

3. Share an example of unexamined power in your life or community. What is the result?

4. Have you read something by an author in the Majority World? Describe any influence it/they had on your life.

5. What would it look like to make minority leaders equal and empowered in the organizations you are part of?

6. Can you think of an example of a transnational friendship taking off your blinders?

7. How do American blinders block greater Christian maturity, and what steps might help you grow in becoming a transnational disciple of Christ?

6. PURSUING PRIVATE INTEGRITY FOR A WORLD OF PUBLIC VALIDATION

1. Have you ever experienced a crisis that made you newly aware of regrets, broken relationships, or grief?

2. How does this speak to you?: "God's reconciliation is never bigger than the person nearest to you who is most difficult to love."

3. Has a disruption in your life ever become a divine interruption? What did you learn?

4. Have you ever experienced a tension between public validation and private integrity?

5. Have you seen an example of power without communal safeguarding?

6. Have you ever experienced or heard of an organization that faced its failures in a transparent or public way? What was the impact on that organization?

7. "At many times, the faithful movement of Christian maturity in our lives is not from good to great, but from great to little." How does that speak to your own life?

For personal reflection

8. Use the following questions to guide a time of interior examination: What are you mad about? Sad about? Anxious about? Glad about? Discuss your answers with a trusted friend, voice them to God, or reflect with a mentor.

9. Regarding a situation that disturbed you: What happened? What am I feeling? What is the story I'm telling myself? What does the gospel say? What counterinstinctual action is needed?

7. CULTIVATING MORAL IMAGINATION FOR A WORLD OF UNPRECEDENTED DANGERS

1. Of the three dangers discussed in this chapter, which do you think is the most pressing and why?

2. What is the difference between technical solutions and moral imagination? Why is the difference important?

3. Reflect on the story of DRC, cobalt, the battle for dominance between the United States and China, and how cobalt benefits you. How does such a story matter for the church? How does it speak to ways we could change?

4. With the entire chapter in mind, how do you think the gifts of technology, the natural world and its resources, and the national good are being misused in our time or deformed by the lure of domination? How is your life or community being influenced by this?

5. What Think Little remedies in this chapter speak most strongly to you?

8. RENEWING THE CHURCH FOR A WORLD LONGING FOR HOPE

1. What does it mean that renewals need renewing? Can you think of an example?

2. Which of the six essentials in this chapter do you think is most important? Why? And how could you and your community embrace it?

3. When it comes to renewal in the world, what does Christianity bring to the table that is unique, compelling, and precious?

4. "A kind of Christianity that no longer needs the power of Christ cannot renew the church." What does the author mean? Do you agree? Why or why not?

5. What are the implications of the truth that Jesus is our friend? With regard to the challenges in this book and this time in our world, what gifts does his friendship offer that are unique from his gifts as prophet, priest, and king?

EPILOGUE: REST FOR RESTLESS HEARTS

1. Has this book changed your understanding of renewal in your life, community, church, or world? If so, how?

2. If you were to sketch out a pathway of renewal for your community (school, church, town), what would be two or three of the most important elements?

3. What are your most important takeaways from reading this book? What new insights has it given you into what is going on in our world? What have you learned about yourself?

Notes

INTRODUCTION: RENEWING A SHAKEN WORLD

[1] Gallup, *Global Emotions 2022 Report*, 2022, www.gallup.com/analytics/349280/gallup-global-emotions-report.aspx.

[2] "Stress in America™ 2020: A National Mental Health Crisis," American Psychological Association, created October 2020, www.apa.org/news/press/releases/stress/2020/report-october.

[3] The 2020 Intergovernmental Platform on Biodiversity and Ecosystem Services Workshop, an independent body of experts from more than 130 countries, found that five new human diseases are emerging every year, any one of which has the potential to spread globally. They also warned that an estimated 1.7 million currently undiscovered viruses are thought to exist in mammals and birds. Of these, up to half may have the ability to infect humans. "Reduce Risk to Avert 'Era of Pandemics,' Experts Warn in New Report," UN News, October 29, 2020, https://news.un.org/en/story/2020/10/1076392.

[4] Interview with Stanley Hauerwas on Mars Hill Audio, "Quarantined Resident Alien," April 17, 2020.

[5] J. R. R. Tolkien, *The Lord of the Rings: The Fellowship of the Ring* (United Kingdom: HarperCollins Publishers, 2009).

1. BEARING JOY FOR A WORLD OF FRANTIC ANXIETY

[1] Ann Helen Petersen, *Can't Even: How Millennials Became the Burnout Generation* (Boston: Mariner Books, 2020), xx.

[2] Byung-Chul Han, *The Burnout Society* (Stanford, CA: Stanford University Press, 2015), 1.

[3] John Calvin, *Institutes of the Christian Religion* (Peabody, MA: Hendrickson Publishers, 2008), 4.17.36.

[4] Shane Croucher, "America Is More Stressed Than Venezuela, Gallup Poll Shows," *Newsweek*, April 26, 2019, www.newsweek.com/gallup-poll-america-stress-venezuela-mental-health-1406758.

[5] Han, *The Burnout Society*, 11.

[6] Thomas Merton, *Conjectures of a Guilty Bystander* (New York: Doubleday, 1965), 73.

[7] Han, *The Burnout Society*, 11.

[8] Some of this material is drawn from my article "Born Again . . . Again," *Christianity Today*, March 2010, www.christianitytoday.com/ct/2010/march/24.34.html.

[9] Walter Isaacson, "In Search of the Real Bill Gates," *Time*, January 13, 1997, https://content.time.com/time/magazine/article/0,9171,1120657,00.html.

[10] Flannery O'Connor, *The Habit of Being* (New York: Farrar, Straus and Giroux, 1979), 307.

[11] Rich Villodas, *The Deeply Formed Life: Five Transformative Values to Root Us in the Way of Jesus* (New York: Waterbrook, 2020), 3.

[12] Han, *The Burnout Society*, 34.

[13] Evelynne Reisacher, *Joyful Witness in the Muslim World* (Grand Rapids, MI: Baker Academic, 2016).

[14] Barbara A. Holmes, *Joy Unspeakable*: *Contemplative Practices of the Black Church*, 2nd ed. (Minneapolis, MN: Fortress Press, 2017), 126-27.

[15] Lesslie Newbigin, *The Gospel in a Pluralist Society* (Grand Rapids, MI: Eerdmans, 1989), 116.

2. CENTERING THE VULNERABLE FOR A WORLD OF RISING DISPARITY

[1] Yuval Noah Harari, *Twenty-One Lessons for the Twenty-First Century* (New York: Random House, 2018), chap. 4, Kindle.

[2] Kenneth E. Bailey, *Jesus Through Middle Eastern Eyes* (Downers Grove, IL: InterVarsity Press), 288.

[3] Bailey, *Jesus Through Middle Eastern Eyes*, 295.

[4] Yuval Noah Harari on Covid-19: "The biggest danger is not the virus itself," Deutsche Welle (DW), April 22, 2020, www.dw.com/en/virus-itself-is-not-the-biggest-danger-says-yuval-noah-harari/a-53195552.

[5] Vinoth Ramachandra, "The Virus of Fear," blog post, March 17, 2020, https://vinothramachandra.wordpress.com/2020/03/17/the-virus-of-fear.

[6] Bailey, *Jesus Through Middle Eastern Eyes*, 294.

[7] Orlando Patterson, "The Long Reach of Racism in the U.S.," *Wall Street Journal*, June 5, 2020, www.wsj.com/articles/the-long-reach-of-racism-in-the-u-s-11591372542.

[8] Orlando Patterson, "Why American Can't Escape Its Racist Roots," interview by Liz Mineo, *Harvard Gazette*, June 4, 2020, https://news.harvard.edu

/gazette/story/2020/06/orlando-patterson-explains-why-america-cant-escape-its-racist-roots.

9 Charles M. Blow, "Allies, Don't Fail Us Again," *New York Times*, June 7, 2020, www.nytimes.com/2020/06/07/opinion/white-privilege-civil-rights.html.

10 Andy Crouch, *Playing God: Redeeming the Gift of Power* (Downers Grove, IL: InterVarsity Press, 2013), 154.

11 Martin Luther King Jr., "Beyond Vietnam," April 4, 1967, www2.hawaii.edu/~freeman/courses/phil100/17.%20MLK%20Beyond%20Vietnam.pdf.

12 Mark Noll, *The New Shape of World Christianity* (Downers Grove, IL: IVP Academic, 2009), 58-59.

13 Patterson, "The Long Reach of Racism."

14 Jemar Tisby, *The Color of Compromise* (Grand Rapids, MI: Zondervan, 2019), 176.

15 Tisby, *The Color of Compromise*, 184.

16 See chapter five, "The Discipline of Lament," in Emmanuel Katongole and Chris Rice, *Reconciling All Things: A Christian Vision for Justice, Peace, and Healing* (Downers Grove, IL: InterVarsity Press, 2008).

17 The story of Ann Atwater and C. P. Ellis is told in the book by Osha Gray Davidson, *Best of Enemies: Race and Redemption in the New South* (Chapel Hill: University of North Carolina Press, 2019).

18 Emma Green, "The Unofficial Racism Consultants to the White Evangelical Community," *Atlantic*, July 5, 2020, www.theatlantic.com/politics/archive/2020/07/white-evangelicals-black-lives-matter/613738.

19 Stevenson tells his story in his book: Bryan Stevenson, *Just Mercy: A Story of Justice and Redemption* (New York: One World, 2014).

20 Michelle Alexander, "Mass Incarceration in America, Then and Now," interview with David Remick, *New Yorker Radio Hour*, December 3, 2021, www.newyorker.com/podcast/the-new-yorker-radio-hour/mass-incarceration-in-america-then-and-now.

21 "Deep Common Journey Partners," Blacknall Presbyterian Church, https://blacknall.org/deep-common-journey.

22 Harari, *Twenty-One Lessons*, chap. 3.

23 King, "Beyond Vietnam."

24 David Brooks, "How to Do Reparations Right: It's Time to Tackle Racial Disparities," *New York Times*, June 4, 2020, www.nytimes.com/2020/06/04/opinion/united-states-reparations.html.

[25] David Brooks, "America is Facing 5 Epic Crises All at Once," *New York Times*, June 25, 2020, www.nytimes.com/2020/06/25/opinion/us-coronavirus -protests.html.

3. BEING PEACEMAKERS FOR A WORLD OF SURGING POLARIZATION

[1] Elie Wiesel, Nobel Prize speech, The Elie Wiesel Foundation for Humanity, December 10, 1986, https://eliewieselfoundation.org/about-elie-wiesel/nobel -prize-speech/.

[2] Chimamanda Ngozi Adichie, "The Danger of a Single Story," TED talk, July 2009, www.ted.com/talks/chimamanda_ngozi_adichie_the_danger_of _a_single_story.

[3] Andrew Walls, "Old Athens and New Jerusalem: Some Signposts for Christian Scholarship in the Early History of Mission Studies," *International Bulletin of Missionary Research* 21, no. 4 (October 1997): 147.

[4] Spencer Perkins, "Playing the Grace Card," *Christianity Today*, July 13, 1998, www.christianitytoday.com/ct/1998/july13/8t8040.html.

[5] Perkins, "Playing the Grace Card."

[6] Tom Lin, "The Adventurer: Tom Lin," in *Uncommon Ground: Living Faithfully in a World of Difference*, ed. Timothy Keller and John Inazu (Nashville, TN: Nelson Books, 2020), 37.

4. REDEEMING POWER FOR A WORLD OF POLITICAL MEDIOCRITY

[1] Daniel Silliman, "When Is It a Sin to Vote for a Political Candidate?" *Christianity Today*, August 17, 2020, www.christianitytoday.com/ct/2020/september /under-discussion-when-is-it-sin-to-vote-for-political-candi.html.

[2] Aidan Connaughton, "Americans See Stronger Societal Conflicts Than People in Other Advanced Economies," Pew Research Center, www.pewresearch.org /fact-tank/2021/10/13/americans-see-stronger-societal-conflicts-than -people-in-other-advanced-economies; Zoya Wazir, "People See More Social Division After Pandemic," *US News and World Report*, June 23, 2021, www .usnews.com/news/best-countries/articles/2021-06-23/people-across-the -world-say-pandemic-has-increased-social-division.

[3] "38% of U.S. Pastors Have Thought About Quitting Full-Time Ministry in the Past Year," Barna Group, November 16, 2021, www.barna.com/research /pastors-well-being.

[4] Ian Bremmer, "Here's Why America Is So Divided," *Time*, January 16, 2021, https://time.com/5929978/the-u-s-capitol-riot-was-years-in-the-making-heres-why-america-is-so-divided.

[5] Kyle Meyaard-Schaap, "Young Evangelicals are Defying Their Elders' Politics," CNN, September 29, 2020, www.cnn.com/2020/09/29/opinions/young-evangelicals-fight-climate-change-and-trump-meyaard-schaap/index.html.

[6] Carolyn Renée Dupont, "Fannie Lou Hamer's Fight for First Class Citizenship," *Christianity Today*, August 17, 2021, www.christianitytoday.com/ct/2021/september/walk-with-me-larson-fannie-lou-hamer-biography-citizenship.html.

[7] Robert Caro, *Working* (New York: Vintage, 2019), 172.

[8] Caro, *Working*, 179.

[9] Caro, *Working*, 173.

[10] Caro, *Working*, 179.

[11] David Swartz, *Facing West: American Evangelicals in an Age of World Christianity* (New York: Oxford University Press, 2020), 100.

[12] Annette Gordon-Reed and Jon Meacham, "How Could a Slaveholder Write 'All Men Are Created Equal'?" interview by Walter Isaacson, Amanpour & Company, June 26, 2020, www.youtube.com/watch?v=l6vXR5iqReE.

[13] Gordon-Reed and Meacham, "How Could a Slaveholder Write."

[14] Caro, *Working*, 4.

[15] Jonathan Gruber and Simon Johnson, *Jump-Starting America* (New York: Public Affairs, 2019), chap. 4, Kindle.

[16] Caro, *Working*, 199.

[17] Caro, *Working*, 4.

[18] Caro, *Working*, 34.

[19] William Broyles, "The Making of Barbara Jordan," *Texas Monthly*, October 1976, www.texasmonthly.com/news-politics/the-making-of-barbara-jordan-2.

[20] Broyles, "The Making of Barbara Jordan."

[21] Broyles, "The Making of Barbara Jordan."

[22] Broyles, "The Making of Barbara Jordan"; see also "Biography of Barbara Jordan," *History, Art, and Archives*, U.S. House of Representatives, https://history.house.gov/People/Detail/16031.

[23] David Brooks, "Why Partyism is Wrong," *New York Times*, October 27, 2014, www.nytimes.com/2014/10/28/opinion/david-brooks-why-partyism-is-wrong.html.

24 J. I. Packer, "The Bible's Guide for Christian Activism," *Christianity Today*, April 19, 1985, reprinted August 17, 2020, www.christianitytoday.com/ct/2020 /september/j-i-packer-activism-politics-christian-citizenship.html.

25 Bungishabaku Katho, *Reading Jeremiah in Africa: Biblical Essays in Sociopolitical Imagination* (Carlisle, UK: Langham Publishing, 2021), 12.

26 Cass Sunstein, "Partyism," *Chicago Unbound*, University of Chicago Legal Forum, vol. 2015, article 2, https://chicagounbound.uchicago.edu/cgi /viewcontent.cgi?article=1543&context=uclf.

27 Daniel Silliman, "At Purple Churches, Pastors Struggle With Polarized Congregations," *Christianity Today*, October 20, 2020, www.christianitytoday .com/ct/2020/november/purple-church-political-polarization-unity-identity -christ.html.

28 Eugene Cho, "Christians, Stop Being Political Jerks," interview with *Relevant* staff, *Relevant*, November 4, 2021, https://relevantmagazine.com/faith /church/eugene-cho-the-new-president-of-bread-for-the-world-wants -christians-to-stop-being-political-jerks.

29 Brooks, "Why Partyism is Wrong."

30 Brian Stanley, *Christianity in the Twentieth Century* (Princeton, NJ: Princeton University Press, 2018), 169.

31 *Merriam-Webster*, s.v. "retreat," www.merriam-webster.com/dictionary /retreat.

32 Silliman, "When Is It a Sin to Vote for a Political Candidate?"

33 Stanley, *Christianity in the Twentieth Century*, 170.

34 Esau McCaulley, *Reading While Black* (Downers Grove, IL: IVP Academic, 2020), 49.

35 Eugene Cho, "Does Faithfulness Require Political Advocacy?" interview by Jim Wallis, *Sojourners*, 2020, https://sojo.net/media/does-faithfulness-require -political-advocacy-conversation-eugene-cho.

36 Packer, "The Bible's Guide for Christian Activism."

37 Swartz, *Facing West*, 55.

38 Tish Harrison Warren, "The Early Church Saw Itself as a Political Body. We Can Too," *Christianity Today*, October 22, 2020, www.christianitytoday.com /ct/2020/october-web-only/election-politics-president-trump-early-church -model.html.

39 César García, *What Is God's Kingdom and What Does Citizenship Look Like?* (Harrisonburg, VA: Herald Press, 2021), 40.

40 Bungishabaku Katho, interview with Chris Rice, *MCC UN Global Briefing*, February 24, 2022, https://mcc.org/stories/author-interview-bungishabaku-katho.

41 Katho, interview with Rice.

42 John Stott, *Issues Facing Christians Today*, 4th ed. (Grand Rapids, MI: Zondervan, 2006), 34.

43 Stott, *Issues Facing Christians Today*, 35.

44 Martin Luther King Jr., "Where Do We Go From Here?," Annual Report Delivered at the 11th Convention of the Southern Christian Leadership Conference, August 16, 1967, Atlanta, GA, www-personal.umich.edu/~gmarkus /MLK_WhereDoWeGo.pdf.

45 Learn more by listening to "Town Meeting," a half-hour show in the award-winning podcast *Rumblestrip*, https://rumblestripvermont.com/2021/02 /town-meeting.

5. MAKING TRANSNATIONAL DISCIPLES FOR A WORLD OF AMERICAN BLINDERS

1 Martin Luther King Jr., "Beyond Vietnam," April 4, 1967, www2.hawaii .edu/~freeman/courses/phil100/17.%20MLK%20Beyond%20Vietnam.pdf.

2 King, "Beyond Vietnam."

3 Andy Crouch, *Playing God: Redeeming the Gift of Power* (Downers Grove, IL: InterVarsity Press, 2013), 154.

4 Mark Noll, *The New Shape of World Christianity: How American Experience Reflects Global Faith*, (Downers Grove, IL: IVP Academic, 2013), 59; emphasis mine.

5 David Swartz, "World Vision's Forgotten Founder," *Christianity Today*, March 16, 2020, www.christianitytoday.com/ct/2020/april/world-vision-kyung -chik-han-forgotten-founder.html.

6 David Swartz, *Facing West: American Evangelicals in an Age of World Christianity* (New York: Oxford University Press, 2020), 108.

7 Adrian Pei, *The Minority Experience: Navigating Emotional and Organizational Realities* (Downers Grove, IL: InterVarsity Press, 2018), 126.

8 António Gutteres, "Tackling the Inequality Pandemic: A New Social Contract for a New Era," United Nations, July 18, 2020, www.un.org/en/coronavirus /tackling-inequality-new-social-contract-new-era.

9 "The 100 Largest U.S. Charities: 2021 Ranking," *Forbes*, www.forbes.com/top -charities/list/#tab:rank.

10 The annual income of Mennonite Central Committee, the agency where I serve, is no small amount—nearly $100 million.

11 Christopher Scheitle, *Beyond the Congregation: The World of Christian Nonprofits* (New York: Oxford University Press, 2010), 256.

[12] Andy Crouch, *Playing God: Redeeming the Gift of Power* (Downers Grove, IL: InterVarsity Press, 2013), 73-75.

[13] King, "Beyond Vietnam."

[14] Quoted in Chris Rice, "The Pandemic: Where is Moral Leadership?" MCC UN Office, August 31, 2020, https://mcc.org/stories/inequality-pandemic-where -moral-leadership.

[15] For some of their blogs and writings see Vinoth Ramachandra, https://vinoth ramachandra.wordpress.com; Emmanuel Katongole, Africa Matters, https:// emmanuelkatongole.org/; César García, MennoMedia, www.mennomedia .org/author/cesar-garcia/; Aldrin M. Peñamora and Bernard K. Wong, *Asian Christian Ethics*, https://langhamliterature.org/asian-christian-ethics; and "Liberate My People," interview by Andy Crouch, *Christianity Today*, www .christianitytoday.com/ct/2007/august/12.30.html.

[16] One survey of governing boards of prominent international humanitarian NGOs found that fewer than 20 percent of board members were from countries that are eligible to receive aid; see Rose Worden and Patrick Saez, "Shifting Power in Humanitarian Nonprofits: A Review of 15 NGO Governing Boards," Center for Global Development, June 22, 2021, www.cgdev.org /publication/Shifting-Power-in-Humanitarian-Nonprofits-A-Review-of -15-NGO-Governing-Boards.

[17] Pei, *The Minority Experience*, 164.

[18] Pei, *The Minority Experience*, 117-18.

[19] Dana Robert, *Faith Friendships: Embracing Diversity in Christian Community* (Grand Rapids, MI: Eerdmans, 2019), 106.

[20] Robert, *Faith Friendships*, 106.

[21] Members of the Monday Night Group collectively tell their story in Jim Stentzel, ed., *More Than Witnesses: How a Small Group of Missionaries Aided Korea's Democratic Revolution* (Seoul: Korea Democracy Foundation, 2006).

6. PURSUING PRIVATE INTEGRITY FOR A WORLD OF PUBLIC VALIDATION

[1] "38% of U.S. Pastors Have Thought About Quitting Full-Time Ministry in the Past Year," Barna Group, November 16, 2021, www.barna.com/research /pastors-well-being.

[2] Peter Chin, "I've Reached My Breaking Point as a Pastor," *Christianity Today*, February 2, 2022, www.christianitytoday.com/ct/2022/january-web-only /covid-church-pastor-quit-ministry-burnout-breaking-point.html.

3 Peter Scazzero, *Emotionally Healthy Spirituality* (Grand Rapids, MI: Zondervan, 2014), 49-53.

4 Henri Nouwen, *In the Name of Jesus: Reflections on Christian Leadership* (New York: Crossroad, 1989), chap. 1, Kindle.

5 Nouwen, *In the Name of Jesus*, chap. 1.

6 David Brooks, *The Second Mountain* (New York: Random House, 2020), xx.

7 *Summary Report from L'Arche International*, L'Arche USA, February 22, 2020, www.larcheusa.org/news_article/summary-report-from-larche -international.

8 Ellen Davis, *Getting Involved with God* (Plymouth, UK: Cowley Publications, 2001), chap. 1, Kindle.

9 Davis, *Getting Involved with God*, chap. 1.

10 Davis, *Getting Involved with God*, chap. 2.

11 Davis, *Getting Involved with God*, chap. 1.

12 Davis, *Getting Involved with God*, chap. 14.

13 Dag Hammarskjöld, *Markings* (New York: Knopf, 1964), 55.

14 Rich Villodas, *The Deeply Formed Life: Five Transformative Values to Root Us in the Way of Jesus* (New York: Waterbrook, 2020).

15 See Villodas, *The Deeply Formed Life*, 125; and Peter Scazzero and Geri Scazzero, *Emotionally Healthy Relationships Workbook* (Grand Rapids, MI: Zondervan, 2017), 82.

16 Chin, "I've Reached My Breaking Point as a Pastor."

17 See "Safeguarding," L'Arche USA, www.larcheusa.org/about/safeguarding.

18 Nancy J. Duff, "Recovering Lament as a Practice in the Church," in Sally A. Brown and Patrick Miller, editors, *Lament: Reclaiming Practices in Pulpit, Pew, and Public Square* (Louisville, KY: Westminster John Knox Press, 2005), 4.

19 I write from my personal participation in InterVarsity's institute experience.

20 Paula Fuller, "One Woman's Journey of Lament," 2010 Summer Institute, http://vimeo.com/14248639.

21 Hammarskjöld, *Markings*, 133.

7. CULTIVATING MORAL IMAGINATION FOR A WORLD OF UNPRECEDENTED DANGERS

1 Peter Robinson, "Introduction: A Computer Technology Perspective," in *The Robot Will See You Now*, ed. John Wyatt and Stephen N. Williams (London: SPCK Publishing, 2021), introduction, Kindle.

2 "Facebook Whistleblower Testifies on Children & Social Media Use: Full Senate Hearing Transcript," @rev, blog, October 5, 2021, www.rev.com/blog/transcripts

/facebook-whistleblower-frances-haugen-testifies-on-children-social-media
-use-full-senate-hearing-transcript.

[3] Anna Lembke, "Digital Addictions are Drowning in Dopamine," *Wall Street Journal*, August 14–15, 2021, C3.

[4] Vinoth Ramachandra, "The New Warfare," blog post, July 28, 2021, https://vinothramachandra.wordpress.com/2021/07/28/the-new-warfare.

[5] Bonnie Kristian, "Can Scripture Compete with Scrolling," *Christianity Today*, April 2021, 26.

[6] "Living Planet Report 2020," World Wildlife Fund, 2020, https://f.hubspot
usercontent20.net/hubfs/4783129/LPR/PDFs/ENGLISH-FULL.pdf.

[7] "Deadly Drought in Kenya Creates Humanitarian Crisis," *PBS NewsHour* video story, January 14, 2022, www.pbs.org/video/kenya-drought-1642200559.

[8] Vinoth Ramachandra, "Beyond the Vaccine," blog post, December 29, 2020, https://vinothramachandra.wordpress.com/2020/12/29/beyond
-the-vaccine.

[9] Myrrl Byler, "Why the Call to Peacemaking Must Not Ignore China," interview with Chris Rice, MCC UN Office Global Briefing, 26, 2021, https://mcccanada
.ca/stories/myrrl-byler-why-call-peacemaking-must-not-ignore-china.

[10] Matthew Taylor King, "The Gospel According to Xi," *Wall Street Journal*, June 4, 2020, www.wsj.com/articles/the-gospel-according-to-xi-11591310956.

[11] Mohamed Younis, "New High in Perceptions of China as U.S.'s Greatest Enemy," Gallup, March 16, 2021, https://news.gallup.com/poll/337457/new
-high-perceptions-china-greatest-enemy.aspx.

[12] "Stop AAPI Hate National Report," March 17, 2020, to December 31, 2021, https://stopaapihate.org/wp-content/uploads/2022/03/22-SAH
-NationalReport-3.1.22-v9.pdf.

[13] "Asian Americans Battling Bias: Continuing Crisis," CBS one-hour special program, March 31, 2021, www.cbsnews.com/video/asian-americans-battling
-bias-continuing-crisis.

[14] Dionne Searcey, Michael Forsythe, and Eric Lipton, "A Power Struggle Over Cobalt Rattles the Energy Revolution," *New York Times*, November 20, 2021, www.nytimes.com/2021/11/20/world/china-congo-cobalt.html.

[15] Ellen F. Davis, "Meaning of Dominion," *Passages,* Bible Odyssey, April 16, 2022, www.bibleodyssey.org/passages/related-articles/the-meaning-of
-dominion/.

[16] John Paul Lederach, *The Moral Imagination: The Art and Soul of Building Peace* (New York: Oxford University Press, 2005), vii-ix.

[17] Quoted in Wendell Berry, *Think Little* (Berkeley: Counterpoint, 2019), Kindle.

18 Randy Woodley, *Indigenous Theology and the Western Worldview: A Decolonized Approach to Christian Doctrine* (Grand Rapids, MI: Baker, 2022).

19 Davis, "Meaning of Dominion."

20 Translation is by Ellen Davis. This and references following from Ellen Davis, "Becoming Human: Biblical Interpretation and Ecological Responsibility," Kreitler Lecture, Virginia Theological Seminary, April 22, 2008.

21 David Marchese, "Why Jane Goodall Still Has Hope for Us Humans," *New York Times Magazine*, July 12, 2021, www.nytimes.com/interactive/2021/07/12/magazine/jane-goodall-interview.html.

22 Two pioneers of the concept of "wicked problems" are design theorists Horst Rittel and Melvin Webber. See H. W. Rittel, and M. M. Webber, "Dilemmas in a General Theory of Planning," *Policy Sciences* 4, no. 2 (1973): 155-69, www.stonybrook.edu/commcms/wicked-problem/about/What-is-a-wicked-problem.php.

23 Berry, *Think Little.*

24 Berry, *Think Little.*

25 Byler, "Why the Call to Peacemaking."

26 Byler, "Why the Call to Peacemaking."

27 Learn more at Stop AAPI Hate, stopaapihate.org.

28 Peggy Noonan, "How to Protect Children from Big Tech Companies," *Wall Street Journal*, April 7, 2022, www.wsj.com/articles/can-anyone-tame-big-tech-social-media-algorithms-addiction-data-privacy-11649367343.

29 Doris Kearns Goodwin, *Leadership in Turbulent Times* (New York: Simon and Schuster, 2018), 225.

30 Berry, *Think Little.*

31 Eliza Griswold, "How to Talk About Climate Change Across the Political Divide," *New Yorker*, September 16, 2021, www.newyorker.com/news/on-religion/how-to-talk-about-climate-change-across-the-political-divide.

32 Griswold, "How to Talk About Climate Change Across Political Divides."

8. RENEWING THE CHURCH FOR A WORLD LONGING FOR HOPE

1 Kimberly Deckel, "Love at the Center," *Christianity Today*, Spring 2022, 64.

2 Ross Douthat, "Can Politics Save Christianity?" *New York Times*, December 18, 2021, www.nytimes.com/2021/12/18/opinion/christianity-politics.html.

3 David Brooks, "The Dissenters Trying to Save Evangelicalism From Itself," *New York Times*, February 4, 2022, www.nytimes.com/2022/02/04/opinion/evangelicalism-division-renewal.html.

[4] Emily McFarlan Miller and Adelle M. Banks, "#PandemicPastoring Report Documents a 'New Era in Ministry,'" Religion News Service, September 1, 2022, https://religionnews.com/2022/09/01/pandemicpastoring-report -documents-a-new-era-in-ministry.

[5] Brooks, "The Dissenters."

[6] Quoted in Charles Marsh, *The Beloved Community: How Faith Shapes Social Justice, From the Civil Rights Movement to Today* (New York: Basic Books, 2005), 1.

[7] Vinoth Ramachandra, "Seeds of Hope?" blog post, December 31, 2019, https:// vinothramachandra.wordpress.com/2019/12/31/seeds-of-hope.

[8] Brooks, "The Dissenters."

[9] Brooks, "The Dissenters."

[10] Sheryl Fullerton, "The Wonderful Ordinariness of Congregational Life," *Christian Century*, March 31, 2022, www.christiancentury.org/article/first -person/wonderful-ordinariness-congregational-life.

[11] Collin Hansen, "What We Lose When We Livestream Church," *New York Times*, August 8, 2021, www.nytimes.com/2021/08/08/opinion/covid-church -livestream.html.

[12] "Pope: The Church Is Not an NGO," *Asia News*, April 24, 2018, www.asianews .it/news-en/Pope:-The-Church-is-not-an-NGO-and-the-IOR-is-needed-up-to -a-certain-point-27746.html.

[13] Karl Vaters, "Ministry Over Metrics: Numbers Aren't the Only Way to Determine Church Health. In Fact, They're Not Even the Best Way," *Christianity Today*, April 16, 2022.

[14] Tish Harrison Warren, "Why Churches Should Drop Their Online Worship," *New York Times*, January 30, 2022, www.nytimes.com/2022/01/30/opinion /church-online-services-covid.html.

[15] Andrew Walls, *The Missionary Movement in Christian History: Studies in the Transmission of Faith*, (Maryknoll, NY: Orbis, 1996), 254.

[16] Walls, *The Missionary Movement*, 254.

[17] Walls, *The Missionary Movement*, 79.

[18] The InterVarsity story has been drawn from my interview with Steve Hayner in February 2013 and from Jason Byassee, "Reconciliation on Campus," *Faith & Leadership*, April 2010, www.faithandleadership.com/content/reconciliation -campus; Neil Rendall and Pete Hammond, "The History of InterVarsity's Multiethnic Journey," 2007, http://mem.intervarsity.org/mem/about-mem /history; David Swartz, *Moral Minority: The Evangelical Left in an Age of Conservatism* (Philadelphia: University of Pennsylvania Press, 2012).

[19] African Americans like Tom Skinner and Latin Americans like Samuel Escobar used the Urbana missions conference platform to speak about exclusion, social justice, and the Bible, and made direct critiques of InterVarsity. Writes Jason Byassee, "In his address Skinner said: 'If you have any illusions that America was founded on godly principles, abandon them.' Because white evangelicals had been silent on racism, he said, God had to raise up non-Christian leaders such as Malcolm X to tell blacks that their skin and culture are beautiful," (Byassee, "Reconciliation on Campus").

[20] Walls, *The Missionary Movement*, 254.

[21] I am indebted for some insights in this section provided by Mennonite scholar and practitioner Andrés Pacheco Lozano of Colombia, from reflections he offered on 2 Corinthians 5 at an MCC international program meeting in Cambodia in June 2022.

[22] Robert Westbrook, "How Protestant Missionaries Helped Usher in Post-Protestant America," *Christian Century*, September 13, 2018, www.christian century.org/review/books/how-american-protestant-missionaries-helped -usher-post-protestant-america; emphasis mine.

Also by Chris Rice

More Than Equals
Spencer Perkins and Chris Rice
978-0-8308-4864-5

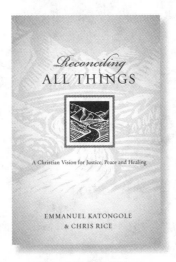

Reconciling All Things
Emmanuel Katongole and Chris Rice
978-0-8308-3451-8